Communicating with Dying People and their Relatives

Jean Lugton

with illustrations by
Stephen Gaffney

Austen Cornish Publishers Limited
in association with
The Lisa Sainsbury Foundation

First published in 1987 by
Austen Cornish Publishers Limited,
Austen Cornish House,
Walham Grove,
London SW6 1QW
in association with
The Lisa Sainsbury Foundation

Reprinted 1988

ISBN 1 870065 034

Printed in Great Britain by MRM Ltd, 322 Oxford Road,
Reading, Berks.

Communicating with Dying People and their Relatives

The Lisa Sainsbury Foundation Series

It is difficult to accept that there comes a time when death is inevitable and that we will all come to the end of life's journey; each of us has needs to be met whether one is the dying person, the carer, a member of the family or a friend. There is now considerable interest in this subject and growing understanding that nurses and other health care professionals need to increase their knowledge and develop their skills further so that they can care more effectively for dying people.

The needs of both the dying person and his or her carers are central to the series, which will provide short and readable books on a wide range of topics, including loss, pain control care, nutritional needs, communication skills, chemotherapy, radiotherapy and caring for dying children and adolescents.

The books are designed to provide nurses and other health care professionals with a resource of knowledge and also with material which should stimulate discussion between colleagues. They can be used independently but will together provide a library covering many different aspects of care each stressing the importance of the needs of the individual person, and the essential part played by good communication skills.

Series Editors

Vera Darling OBE SRN RNT BTA OND is Director of the Lisa Sainsbury Foundation and was, until recently, Associate Lecturer in the Department of Educational Studies at the University of Surrey. Previously, she was Professional Officer for Continuing Education and Training at the English National Board for Nursing, Midwifery and Health Visiting, and before this was Principal Officer at the Joint Board of Clinical Nursing Studies.

Prue Clench MBE SRN is Nurse Adviser on Terminal Care Services. She has a background in Radiotherapy Nursing and developed one of the earliest Macmillan Nursing teams caring for dying people in the community.

Contents

Foreword, vii

Acknowledgements, ix

Introduction, x

1   Terminal illness, 1
     Maintaining hope, 1
     Quality of life, 2
     Sudden death, 6
     Improving communication, 6
     Questions and exercises, 7

2   Needs of staff caring for terminally ill people, 8
     Being prepared for work in terminal care, 10
     Creating time, space and privacy for communication, 11
     Self-awareness in terminal care, 12
     Developing necessary qualities, 13
     Developing realistic expectations, 15
     Developing teamword and receiving support, 16
     Questions and exercises, 18

3   Breaking bad news, 20
     Assessing patients' awareness and reactions, 20
     Assessing coping styles and planning support, 21
     Looking for cues, 28
     Potential problem areas, 28
     Questions and exercises, 31

4   Assessing continuing needs for information and
         support, 32
     Understanding fears, 33
     Expectations about treatment and symptom control, 36
     Matching support to the need, 37
     Relatives' needs, 38

Giving sensitive support, 40
Questions and exercises, 41

5   Planning support for family and close friends, 43
     Identifying those needing support, 43
     Family awareness and communication, 44
     Confused patients, 48
     Communicating with children, 50
     Questions and exercises, 53

6   Preparing relatives for bereavement, 55
     Accepting the reality of impending loss, 55
     Experiencing the pain of grief, 56
     Identifying relatives needing extra support, 59
     Adjusting to an environment in which the dying person
       is missing, 61
     Bereavement follow up, 62
     Questions and exercises, 63

7   Making communication more effective, 64
     Non-verbal communication, 65
     Informality: breaking down barriers, 66
     Availability, consistency and counselling skills, 68
     Questions and exercises, 73

8   Potential communication problems, 74
     Poor communication in terminal care, 74
     Obtaining the required support, 80
     Communicating spiritual needs, 81
     Questions and exercises, 82

9   A three-stage model for support in terminal care, 83
     Stage one, 86
     Stage two, 88
     Stage three, 89
     Assessing the level of support needed, 90
     Closing contact, 90
     Questions and exercises, 95

     Postscript, 97

     References, 98

     Useful addresses 101

Foreword

Not long ago the topic of death and dying was taboo in the United Kingdom. Recently, more people have become aware that the suffering of the bereaved is greatly increased if they fail to express their grief and that patients can be helped to a better death if they are encouraged to talk about their feelings. It is not easy, however, either for the dying patient, or for the distressed friend or relative, or for the professional care giver, to communicate about dying and to allow their stoic defences to break down.

Nurses and others who are involved in the care of people who are approaching death are aware of their responsibility to communicate with patients and with those who are preparing, with anxiety and sadness, to cope with their imminent loss. Training has not always prepared professionals adequately to cope with the stresses of communicating about death.

In this book, Jean Lugton offers readers the benefit of her personal and professional experience. She supports her views with the statements of many of the relatives of hospice patients who were interviewed in the course of her research.

To hear patients and relatives talking about their experiences at the time when they felt most vulnerable and most in need of comfort, makes a powerful impact on those who are able to listen. But nurses are also distressed and vulnerable at those moments and may need to protect their own emotional stability by appearing detached, calm and composed. Careful reading of this book will help them to examine, in advance and in a non-stressful situation, their own attitudes and their own strengths and weaknesses in facing the problem of dying.

Researchers have taught us that it is necessary to work through the stages of loss and mourning in order to reach a satisfactory outcome of final acceptance. Professionals who have not themselves either directly experienced or worked through these stages will find it difficult to provide the right quality of care for their clients. This book, I believe, gives the professional reader a sound basis to inform their nursing practice. Not only nurses and other professional carers but also patients and their relatives will be glad that this book has been written.

Annie T. Altschul CBE, FRCN
Emeritus Professor of Nursing Studies
University of Edinburgh

Acknowledgements

I should like to thank Meg Bond and Helen McKinnon for their constructive comments on the first draft of this book, and Elizabeth Horne of Austen Cornish Publishers Ltd. for her realism and understanding of the pressures involved in producing what follows. To Stephen Gaffney, a particular word of thanks for his insightful illustrations which use humour to make serious points. I am grateful to Professor Annie Altschul for her perceptive comments on my research and for writing the Foreword to this book. I would also like to thank St Columba's Hospice for the opportunity to bring the findings of my research to a wider audience.

To Trisha Martin go my thanks for reducing my much annotated drafts to very high quality typescript. Finally, I should like to thank my husband, Jim, for his help and understanding while I have been busy writing.

To preserve confidentiality, the names in this book are not those of the people concerned.

A note on the series style

Throughout this book we have used the female gender for nurses of both sexes and the male gender for patients of both sexes, unless specific examples require otherwise. The Publishers and the Author do not in any way wish to offend or discriminate against male nurses or female patients but have chosen to use this convention to avoid the cumbersome use of the genders wherever a nurse or a patient is mentioned. We have chosen this convention because, at present the majority of nurses in the UK are women.

We would also like readers to extend the term "relatives" to include "close friends" where appropriate in discussion throughout the book.

Introduction

There can be few times in life when people are as vulnerable as when they are terminally ill, and yet, paradoxically, because they remind others of their own mortality or that of their nearest and dearest, dying people sometimes pose a threat to those around them. Terminally ill people can be hurt or helped in so many ways by professionals and by their relatives and friends as they struggle to cope not only with their own emotions, but with the attitudes of those around them. The care of a dying person can be a time of self-revelation for professionals when it is difficult to conceal feelings of ineffectiveness, or personal fear about dying. It is also a time of honesty for relatives and friends as they may become conscious of feelings about the dying person, or aspects of their relationship with him which were submerged in the humdrum circumstances of everyday life.

As professionals, we all have memories of caring for a dying person and probably most of us have at some time been left with a sense of inadequacy about our own role in such caring. Perhaps we remember patients being moved into single rooms or positions at the end of a ward. We remember struggling to find words to comfort a distressed patient or anxious, weeping relatives. We sense that our own attitude to terminal care is important in our ability to relate to dying patients and their relatives, yet there is little opportunity to discuss and evaluate our support of a particular patient and family with colleagues, so that we can improve our care in the future. In this book, I hope to share with readers some of my own insights and experiences in working with dying people and their relatives over eight years at St Columba's Hospice. I hope that this sharing of ideas about communications in terminal care will prove helpful to others working within and outside a hospice setting, while always recognising that each person will rightly develop her own approach and her own style of communication.

My own attitudes to death and to terminal care have evolved over time, influenced by events in both my personal and professional life. The most profound influences have been the deaths of some of my close relatives and friends. For one friend, hospital became home as he was too ill to be discharged to care for himself. Being in such an environment for several weeks could have been extremely depressing, but because of the efforts of the staff and the courage of my friend, it was not so. He spoke frequently to the medical staff who managed to encourage him, despite his steadily deteriorating health. A social worker helped with financial problems and arranged a bus pass to enable him to travel to teach the accordion classes he loved. The chaplain visited. The nurses spent time talking to him and to his relatives and planned a small party to celebrate his birthday. The philosophy of good terminal care can be applied in a variety of settings as is most appropriate to the person concerned and to his family.

This book is concerned with communications in terminal care, an area which is potentially stressful to patients, relatives and professionals. I believe that a counselling approach to such communications is essential since this enables people to become more aware of their feelings and the options open to them and to come to terms in their own ways with what is happening to them. The book will begin, therefore, with the needs of nurses for self-understanding and awareness and for support from colleagues as a prerequisite to helping dying patients. It will then consider how patients and relatives can help us to assess their needs for information and support and how and when such information and help should be given. Family members and close friends are under great stress during a patient's terminal illness and their needs at this time, and in preparation for bereavement, are considered.

Some of the practical skills involved in communicating with dying people and their families are described and opportunities to relate these to personal experiences are given in the exercises concluding each chapter. Potential communications problems are discussed. Finally, a model for support of terminally ill people and their relatives is developed, using the skills described in earlier chapters.

Terminal illness

A terminal illness may be defined as one for which no cure is available and which will bring about the death of the person in the fairly near future. However, it is not always easy to recognise when the terminal phase of an illness has been reached. Our care of the dying begins at the time of the fatal diagnosis and not just within the last weeks or days of life.

Patients and their relatives need support and counselling to enable them to cope with the shattering impact of the diagnosis, whether they are asked to face it immediately, or whether it comes as a slowly dawning realisation. It is, therefore, more helpful to speak about 'palliative care' than 'terminal care'.

Palliative care implies actively endeavouring to relieve physical, psychosocial, and spiritual distress and presents great challenges to the carers in the difficult areas of treatment and communication.

Quality of life, not quantity, becomes the aim of care. Knowledge of how people relate to their experience of illness is more important than information about the particular disease which will cause them to die. People can be encouraged to live 'actively' until their last days rather than becoming depressed and resigned to their fate. When a terminal illness has been diagnosed, there may be a temptation by nurses and relatives to overprotect the person, thus preventing him or her from leading as full a life as possible.

MAINTAINING HOPE

A terminal illness is often described as a 'hopeless' situation, yet despairing attitudes about the effectiveness of treatment or about the person's ability to respond to the knowledge of impending death may mean that avenues for the relief of distressing symptoms are not fully explored, or that communications with the family or with health care professionals are blocked. It is important to maintain the delicate balance between realistic hope and acceptance of the inevitable in terminal care. Dying people and their relatives need encouragement to believe that symptoms can be controlled or alleviated even when the disease is incurable, that dignity can be maintained and that they themselves will have the courage as well as support from professionals to enable them to cope with a crisis.

This can only be achieved in an atmosphere of honesty and trust between patients, relatives, and professionals. When people are given misleading information, or when information is withheld from them, they often reach their own conclusions about the true state of affairs from what their bodies are telling them and from their reflections on what has not been said. Paradoxically, total truth may not be very helpful either, since emphasising only the terminal nature of the illness and not the treatment and care that are still available may drive dying people and their relatives to complete despair.

QUALITY OF LIFE

The experience of the hospice movement has shown that terminally ill people can have a fairly good quality of life in the time left to them if their own attitudes and those of the caring professionals remain positive. Relatives can be left with memories of hopes and love shared because communication has been open and honest. Dying people, often even more so than relatives, have great fears of losing dignity and of not coping and they need the reassurance of knowing that professional staff will not be afraid to listen to their fears and to be available to them throughout the illness, even when they cannot solve all the problems. A relative of a hospice patient described his anxieties about his mother's terminal illness:

'From my point of view, home care was a load off my mind
because I had visions of me struggling away with her lying
dying in bed and me trying to cope with it. I imagined the
hospice would be an austere place with people lying in bed
and moaning and that sort of thing, and shouting out. It's
not like that at all.'

The son quoted above went on to describe how his mother enjoyed her visits from home to the day hospice where patients can become involved in a variety of activities and, more importantly, receive support from other patients and staff.

'When she was at home, she would sit for ages talking about the day hospice. I would sit and listen to her for a good hour or two. She seemed to enjoy the day hospice. Nine times out of ten there was a lady at the door when she arrived to welcome her. Then there was a wee bunch of flowers when she came away sometimes. These things make a difference.'

Quality of life seems to comprise something more than physical comfort and symptom control. An important element seems to be living 'actively' and positively, until this is genuinely no longer possible. For example, some patients have attended the day hospice one week and enjoyed their time there, but have deteriorated rapidly and died before they could return the following week. Dying people can be encouraged and enabled to do the things they want, whenever possible, to make plans on a day-to-day basis and to celebrate important times such as birthdays and wedding anniversaries. Staff can encourage such planning and the shortness of time that may be left need not be a deterrent. Small things which seem unimportant when someone is terminally ill, may in fact be very important to the person concerned. For example, dentures which no longer fit may increase problems of poor appetite or mouth discomfort. Having a faulty hearing aid quickly repaired may make a great difference to a person's ability to enjoy conversation with his family. People can be encouraged to maintain their social contacts by having flexible visiting hours, and facilities for visitors to have light snacks and a place to relax or stay overnight if they wish. It is sometimes forgotten that being ill at home can be a lonely experience for the patient and the carer. The patient can become increasingly dependent and housebound with the relative unable to leave him alone, as the following example shows:

'When he was in the house, he was sitting in a chair and all he could see was the tops of the tenements opposite. He knew the times of the planes coming over Calton Hill. There was nobody passing. In the hospice, he can see people coming and going and the children playing outside. He can speak to people, whereas in the house there was no conversation at all and latterly the only thing he and my mother could talk about was their experience of hospital.'

Staff can maintain a positive approach to improving a person's quality of life by encouraging patients and their families to make plans. We need to consider whether to take the initiative in suggesting to patients and relatives what can be done in this area. We will, however, only be in a position to do so if we know the patients and their relatives well enough to be aware of their wishes. Individual care and attention is very highly valued by patients and relatives. Relatives like to feel that the patient is special to the staff as well as to themselves as the following comments show:

'The staff here have got a lot more time for individual care and attention. The staff here take time to talk to people and know what's going on.'

'You're making all those patients still remain individuals.'

Patients also express satisfaction with this individualised care and attention and their sense of security is increased by the perceived availability and experience of staff.

'He didn't worry too much about coming here because he'd get more attention, he said. He's quite happy, as happy as you can be.'

'Mother likes it here because it's more relaxed. The staff have got more time for individual care and attention.'

Attention to what may appear to be minor detail is most important in improving a person's sense of well-being. For example, arranging for a hair cut can be a great morale booster. We need to be aware of priorities as determined by the patients, people they wish to see, things they want to do, an important date or event in the future they wish to celebrate. If we are aware of people's priorities, we can help them to use their limited energies and the short time remaining to maximum effect and create some happy memories for relatives. Good communication with dying people and their relatives has to be set in the context of a total relationship between them and the professional carers. The skill of the professional is in being able to establish these relationships in a much shorter timescale than normal. The emphasis must be on the essentials and on being as natural as one would be in forming relationships on a personal rather than a strictly professional basis. Caring attitudes are conveyed in so many ways other than words.

Recognising the dying person

In chronic illness, it is sometimes difficult to know when the terminal phase has been reached. Elderly people may suffer the effects of arteriosclerosis or Alzheimer's disease for many years before they die. This can pose problems for professional carers and severe strains on relatives. Who makes the decisions about therapy, or about the resources which should be used in an endeavour to keep a chronically ill person at home? For the elderly chronically ill, as for any age group, the main consideration is to maintain quality of life for the person and caring relatives. This requires very skilled judgement and ongoing assessment of the medical condition and social circumstances, especially when a person suffers from a number of chronic conditions and the prognosis is uncertain. It is often difficult to steer a middle course between a 'fight to the last' approach and the attitude 'Don't treat anything too energetically in the elderly'.

A myocardial infarction, chest infection or further extension of an existing cerebrovascular accident may increase an existing debility, hasten death or cause sudden death. Dramatic changes in condition will be noticed by everybody, but less marked changes may only be noticed by experienced staff. The difficulties in recognising that a person is dying pose problems for communication and support. The patient may be anxious, yet uncertain of what is happening. It cannot be assumed that an elderly person will more readily accept the prospect of death than someone younger. Relatives may need to be helped to face the probability that the patient will die. They do not always notice or want to believe this. Often the relatives of older patients are elderly themselves and time and care should be taken to explain to them the changes that take place or are likely to occur. Hospital wards are often busy and understaffed and community nurses have heavy caseloads. The needs and feelings of the nursing staff may be overlooked or not considered important, yet they may have invested a lot of themselves in a relationship with a chronically ill patient and family over many months or years.

Younger people with long-term debilitating conditions are another group in whom it may be difficult to recognise that a terminal stage in the illness has been reached. For example, children infected by meningitis may survive the initial illness, against all odds, only to be left severely mentally handicapped. Children with cystic fibrosis are now surviving into their teens and twenties. Parents' hopes for children's recovery may be dashed and raised many times as they survive each crisis. Eventually, parents can become emotionally exhausted. They will need skilled psychological support in the months and years that follow and not just in the acute stages of the child's illness, to enable them to face a future in which they know that sudden deterioration and death can occur at any time.

SUDDEN DEATH

When a person dies suddenly, the shock to relatives and friends will be great. Research has shown that lack of preparation for bereavement can lead to difficulties and a poor outcome. Bereaved people may be so shocked at the time of death that the full emotional impact may not be felt until weeks or months later. A prolonged stage of numbness or denial will make support extremely difficult for both friends and professional carers. It is important that reactions to sudden death are not just accepted at face value. A person who expresses very little emotion at the time may be the one who needs the most help in coming to terms with bereavement later.

Bereaved relatives who may be in a state of shock, should have someone to accompany them home and a relative should not be alone at home when news of death is received. The police have a policy of sending two officers to deliver news of a sudden death, so that one officer can remain with the bereaved person, if necessary, until another friend or relative comes to help. Recent years have seen the formation of self-help groups to support relatives bereaved after cot death, road traffic accidents, the Bradford football stadium fire and the Zeebrugge ferry disaster. This indicates the great needs of the bereaved for continuing understanding and emotional support.

IMPROVING COMMUNICATION

Communication in terminal care constitutes a delicate network of interaction between patients, relatives, and staff. Problems arise if there are failures at any point in the network. Our support to patients and families must be sensitive to their changing needs. We need to know when to remain in the background and when to assume a more positive role. As nurses, we are key people in the support network, often receiving the confidences of patients and meeting relatives on a daily basis. We also have to be aware of the needs of our own colleagues for support in the sometimes stressful task of caring for the terminally ill, giving them opportunities to talk to us and to share their feelings with us. Not infrequently among hospice staff and in groups of nurses and other professionals visiting the hospice on courses, I have found someone painfully reminded of past experience of bereavement or a seriously ill relative.

Working in a team with other professionals is more rewarding when mutual respect, and a readiness to listen to other persons' points of view exist. It is easy, however, to become defensive about professional boundaries and keeping other team members – doctors, community nurses, or clergy – informed, is hard work but essential if the physical, psychosocial and spiritual care of patients and their relatives is not to suffer. Of course, good communication with professional colleagues can greatly increase job satisfaction for nurses.

Questions and Exercises

1. Think back to the last time a patient of yours died suddenly. How did you support the relatives? Which aspects of your support were most effective? In what ways could you have improved your support?
2. How much of your time caring for terminally ill patients do you spend communicating with them? Should such communications be a greater priority for you? How could you improve the priority you attach to communication?
3. In what ways do you distinguish the needs of relatives of terminally ill patients from patients' needs? Which needs of relatives do you think you best meet? Could you further improve your ability to meet those needs?
4. What realistic encouragements can you give dying patients and their relatives to maintain hope and prevent despair?
5. How do you support patients with chronic (terminal) conditions through recurrent crises? Which aspects of your support are most/least effective? In what ways could you improve your support?

Needs of staff caring for 2
terminally ill people

It seems to me that although care of dying people and their relatives can be stressful to the professionals concerned, it can also be very rewarding. Each person's experience of stress in terminal care is different, depending on previous experiences of death or bereavement and established ways of coping with the emotions aroused by stress of any kind. I believe that it is important to have some insight into our feelings and to be able to acknowledge when we are upset, rather than giving the appearance to colleagues and to patients that nothing ever troubles us. Being professional and retaining the ability to support others does not, in my experience, mean being invulnerable to feeling sad or, on occasions, angry.

Stress is not always destructive. At an optimum level it provides stimulation, challenge and incentive to improve standards of care. Terminal care provides just such a challenge to our skills and makes great demands on personal and professional resources. A person who is ill at ease working with the dying may need considerable help and understanding from colleagues to face up to fears which may be subconscious. Hospice staff are not immune to stress arising from their work. Wilson (1985) found that hospice nurses were no more or less susceptible to stress than nurses working in other specialities. Caring for patients' emotional needs was considered by hospice nurses to be more stressful than physical care.

'Nurses were significantly more likely to interact with patients whose needs were purely physical and to give such patients more attention. Patients with emotional needs received significantly less nurse contact which was more likely to be only routine.'

There are, in my experience, very few patients whose needs are purely physical, but there are patients whose psychological needs place considerable demands on staff for support. As nurses, we need to be aware of the distancing strategies we can use in communication to protect ourselves from pain, for example, giving excessive reassurance, talking to other nurses instead of to patients or relatives. We need to be aware of our own attitudes to death and dying.

It is important to recognise that professional helpers, as well as patients and relatives, have needs in terminal care. Some of these needs are as follows:

1. Being adequately prepared for work in terminal care and having the opportunities to gain skills and confidence
2. Having the time, space and privacy to communicate with dying patients and their relatives
3. Developing self-awareness and knowledge of their own attitudes and feelings

4. Developing the qualities necessary for effective relationships with dying patients and relatives
5. Developing realistic expectations of what can be achieved
6. Developing teamwork and receiving support from colleagues

These needs will now be considered in more detail.

BEING PREPARED FOR WORK IN TERMINAL CARE

Inadequate preparation for work in terminal care often results in a lack of confidence on the part of staff. Birch (1979) found that although care of the dying was stressful to student nurses, it was not emphasised in the learning curriculum and that care of the bereaved received even less treatment. Experienced nurses will know only too well that learners often have their first experiences of terminal care in hospitals without adequate preparation and without opportunities to express their feelings to senior colleagues. Physical aspects of

terminal care have hitherto been overstressed in nursing education at the expense of the more difficult task of exploring emotions and attitudes. Attitudes influence every aspect of care – pyschosocial, spiritual or physical. Nurses' attitudes towards pain control and to the use of opiates in terminal care will affect their skills and confidence in monitoring pain and in ensuring that adequate analgesia is given. If the use of opiates is equated with euthanasia, hastening of the patient's death or excessive drowsiness, there will be a reluctance to cooperate fully in using such drugs or in recognising the patient's need for them. Thankfully, education in terminal care is improving but many nurses and other professionals are still underprepared for all aspects of the work.

Terminal care can often be seen as unrewarding to health care professionals because these patients do not get better. Too many doctors and nurses still regard a patient's death as a failure on their part. However, terminal care is increasingly recognised by professionals and by the general public as an area requiring special skills in symptom control and psychological support and there has been a growth of specialist services in the community, hospitals and hospices. Courses in terminal care for the various health care professionals are now well established, research has indicated ways to raise standards, and journal articles and books on the subject are now more readily available. It is possible to develop our skills in communication and support as well as in the physical care of the dying. Counselling courses, specialised and general, of varying lengths and intensity are widely available. For example, CRUSE, a national organisation for the bereaved (see Useful addresses) runs courses for its volunteer counsellors.

CREATING TIME, SPACE AND PRIVACY FOR COMMUNICATION

It is important to create an atmosphere of space and privacy to talk with and listen to dying people and their relatives. At the hospice nurses with a general hospital background often complained that there was nowhere private to go in a busy ward. Often there were frequent interruptions and telephone calls which occurred just at the moment when a patient or relative was trying to express his deepest anxieties and fears. This makes it very difficult to have anything but very hurried and superficial conversations with patients and relatives.

A room apart which provides privacy and freedom from interruptions, can be a great asset and should not be impossible to obtain if there is real concern about giving patients and relatives the opportunities to talk which they have the right to expect. Nurses often feel guilty about spending time in this way because the results of such communications are not always apparent and some of the information may be given in confidence. Two comfortable chairs placed close to each other at a ninety degree angle should enable a patient or relative to feel relaxed. The environment in which we conduct such a discussion should convey the respect we wish to show to the patient or relative. Some hospitals now have rooms which are furnished so that relatives can stay overnight or at least doze in an armchair when visiting a very sick person. This helps to convey a feeling that the needs of the relative are considered to be important to hospital staff. When talking to patients who are in bed, it is better for staff to sit in a chair by the bed so that they are not looking down on the patient or appearing to be in a hurry to get away. At home, there is generally more privacy for patients than in hospital but sometimes a person has too many well-meaning friends and neighbours calling and feels exhausted as a result. The community nurse may have to make tactful suggestions about visiting arrangements that are best for the patient.

SELF-AWARENESS IN TERMINAL CARE

Personal experiences can influence attitudes to work with dying people, e.g. witnessing a painful death, or having a difficult bereavement. Sometimes carers are not aware of how much such an experience still affects them until situations at work remind them of their own loss. The experience of losing a close relative or friend can give staff added insight and sensitivity in working with dying and bereaved people, but it is easy to underestimate personal needs in our anxiety to help others. We need to understand our own emotions and to acknowledge them and to take for ourselves the advice that we often give to the bereaved, not to suppress feelings or pretend that we are always coping.

Dying people and their relatives evoke the normal range of feelings in the staff who are caring for them. Staff may feel unable to express any negative feelings about people because they are dying. This may not be helpful either to patients or their relatives. Bereaved people often feel they can no longer acknowledge the faults and failings of the deceased and this in turn can give rise to feelings of guilt over their own attitudes and behaviour. Relationships within a family can become distorted if relatives feel that the dying person can never be contradicted. The patient may feel unsafe with staff who are 'too kind' since he may feel unable to express his own negative emotions. Nurses should behave as human beings with human emotions and should not be only concerned with appearing clinically correct.

It is important to monitor the development of our skills in supporting the terminally ill and their relatives. Sometimes we are conscious of using these skills, for example, when we have successfully interpreted non-verbal cues as to how a patient is feeling. At other times we are equally conscious of having failed to understand or communicate with them sensitively. It can be very revealing when we assess our interactions with patients and relatives on a day-to-day basis. Discovering our own needs and motivations is an ongoing process, requiring courage and honesty. In this way we build up a picture of our own strengths and weaknesses as communicators. Personal growth can be maintained by willingness to learn from real life situations (a kind of 'critical incident' technique). There are also support and growth groups which provide opportunities to benefit from the insights of others.

Self-awareness is one of the qualities that Carkuff (1969) considered necessary in effective counselling. Other qualities were empathy, genuineness, and unconditional acceptance of others. A climate of trust is created not only by what is said but by the understanding shown in facial expression, tone of voice, and gestures. These demonstrate our confidence in the person and his ability to use his own resources to help himself.

DEVELOPING NECESSARY QUALITIES

For effective relationships with patients and their relatives, a professional and personal approach is required. The personal relationships developed in terminal care, which are essential to giving patients and relatives adequate support, may mean that from time to time we can get overinvolved or identify too closely with a particular patient or relative. Staff can identify strongly with certain patients, e.g. patients of their own age, those who remind them of someone close to them, those with attractive personalities. There is a need to develop such personal relationships with patients in terminal care to understand and support them. The relationship often has within it elements of friendship. The key to effective support is availability and being ready at any time and in any way to respond to the needs of the patient. Many people imagine that care of dying people is always depressing and stressful. A theology student on a course at St Columba's Hospice describes how his views were changed:

'One of my main feelings before working at the hospice was an uneasiness with the presence of death. I did not feel able to cope with the bereaved person, having no idea how to help them. My hospice experience radically altered that. I came to realise that by my contact with the patients, dying was not the catastrophic ending I thought it might be. I learned that care required a large range of responses, the ability to listen, the ability not to interfere, coupled with complete willingness to be available and to be turned away.'

Dying patients, like other people, want us to respond to them in a natural way. They do not want us always to be solemn and are almost always able to share a smile or appreciate a joyful event. Getting close to patients is one of the most rewarding aspects of terminal care, but we cannot mourn the death of each patient as we would that of a close relative or friend. Care should be taken in nursing practice that empathy is not confused with identification. Empathy enables the helper to put herself in another person's position and to recognise how that person may be feeling. Identification means that the helper becomes the other person to the extent of taking on his problems. The patient or relative needs to be helped to work through his own anxieties and problems. Therefore helpers must remain themselves to be effective for patients and relatives and to ensure their own survival.

DEVELOPING REALISTIC EXPECTATIONS

Staff may have unrealistic expectations of what can be accomplished in terminal care. This is the opposite of the attitude 'there's nothing more that can be done'. For example, nurses are often idealistic, committed to their work, and find they are sometimes unable to meet the standards they have set themselves. They may be unable to spend as much time as they would like with patients when short staffed. Nurses from large NHS hospitals or with heavy caseloads in the community, often see the principles of care espoused by the hospice movement as unattainable in their own situation. It is important that nurses' expectations of themselves are realistic, otherwise they may defend themselves from anxiety by remaining emotionally detached from patients and relatives and concentrating on physical care.

In spite of every effort by doctors or nurses, some patients are depressed or have a very poor quality of life. Staff may be disturbed by their apparent inability to control symptoms or give dying patients the emotional support they are seeking. Some patients have a fear of death rather than the experience of dying and can be very difficult to help, as the following hospice examples show.

Example 1
'She's worried about herself, the thought of dying. She
doesn't say much. She keeps a lot to herself. When she sees
the rest of them, she sees a lot of pitiful sights. Every time
they close her door she knows there's another body going
past. She knows that because when she was in hospital one
of the nurses said "I'll have to close the door. It's an old man
that's died." She's frightened. She told the doctor she just
wished it was all over.'

Example 2
'It was a very traumatic business for her to decide to come
in. She knows all too well that this is it in terms of her
illness. She's not happy, but who is happy in the terminal
stages of lung cancer. I don't think it's anything to do with
the hospice, her unhappiness. All the staff are very kind.'

Some people, in the past, have had distressing experiences which make it difficult for them to accept support when it is offered in the last few weeks of life. The concept of 'good enough care' described by Winnicot (1968) in regard to mothering can be helpful in setting realistic expectations for patient care. No mother can hope to meet every need of her baby. In a similar way we cannot meet all the needs of dying patients or overcome all the constraints imposed by our work situations. Acceptance of our limitations will enable us to discard guilt over not being able to solve other peoples' problems. All that we can offer is help to enable patients and relatives to cope better themselves.

DEVELOPING TEAMWORK AND RECEIVING SUPPORT

Nurses can be very unsupported in their care of dying and bereaved people. This lack of support can occur at all levels of the profession, from student nurses to senior staff.

Colleagues can provide valuable opportunities for nurses to talk about their own feelings about, and experiences with, the terminally ill. However, opportunities need to be created if such support is to be available, so team meetings and case conferences are worthwhile in this regard. Support groups may be useful for nurses working in more isolated situations. The psychological privacy of patients and relatives should always be respected and it is not necessary to reveal to the whole team confidences given to a particular staff member who has developed a close relationship with a patient and family.

Junior staff should be given structured opportunities to talk to seniors about their experiences with dying patients and their relatives. It is important that such opportunities are created in the clinical situation as well as in the college. Student nurses may have had distressing personal experiences with death and bereavement which will affect their attitudes to terminal care unless they are given opportunities to share their anxieties and receive adequate support. Senior staff can sometimes act as role models for students, for example, in taking a student with them when talking to a patient or relative, whenever possible.

Lack of defined areas of responsibility for staff involved in terminal care can create role conflicts between professionals and uncertainty and confusion for patients and relatives. For example, nurses may not always be aware of what terminally ill patients and their relatives have been told about the illness by the doctor, making their own supportive role uncertain.

Cultivating mutual respect between professionals is essential if colleagues are to support each other and give support to dying people and their relatives. This may be achieved for example, through regular team meetings, case conferences, and interdisciplinary education which enable the various professionals to see more clearly the contribution each can make and to become more aware of the dilemmas each may encounter at work. Staff are supported when members of the different caring professions share knowledge of what can be achieved in terminal care and are in agreement about the ways in which patients can be helped.

Recognition and support come not only from colleagues but, perhaps surprisingly, from dying people, patients and their relatives. They are, after all, part of the team. They can teach us so much about

the experience of dying and bereavement and often cope with their difficulties with great courage. They encourage us to reflect on the meaning of life and often help us to put our smaller personal problems into perspective. Dying patients are often flatteringly grateful for anything that is done for their well-being. This should not prevent us from always seeking to improve our care.

Some ways in which we can reduce the stress involved in terminal care have been described in this chapter. I believe that we should be prepared to make periodic self-assessments and to review our work with colleagues so that we can maintain a fresh and sensitive approach and develop new skills in this important area. Sometimes frustrations and stresses in terminal care seem to be outwith our control as, for example, in the experience of professional isolation or lack of support from colleagues. It is important to identify the constraints within a situation, but also to be aware of opportunities and possibilities for change. Nurses who have attended courses at St Columba's Hospice have often seen the Hospice as an 'ideal' situation and have pointed out the difficulties of applying the principles of hospice care in their own work settings where they are less well staffed, or where they work with colleagues who do not seem to share their views about terminal care. Many of these nurses have found it productive to consider one or two aspects of terminal care over which they have influence and wish to improve, rather than seeking to make many changes in the short term. For example, a Macmillan nurse decided to concentrate on improving communications between her colleagues and the district nurses in her area. There is in my opinion, almost always something that we can do to improve the care of dying patients and their relatives.

Questions and exercises

1. In what ways have you tried to monitor your communication skills? Would you consider any of the following methods of evaluation helpful?
    (a) tape-recorded/video-recorded interview (e.g. with a colleague).
    (b) discussion of your support of individual patients at a team meeting or case conference.

(c) retrospective self-evaluation of your interactions with particular patients and relatives.
2. Six needs of nurses caring from the terminally ill and their families were mentioned in this chapter. Which of your own needs are best and least met in this area? How could you improve your situation?

In communicating the diagnosis of a terminal illness or a poor prognosis, most medical and nursing staff are likely to have experienced problems. Feelings of inadequacy, concern about the patient's reactions, together with the constraints of team policy on giving information, may result in nurses avoiding rather than facing up to the issues.

ASSESSING PATIENTS' AWARENESS AND REACTIONS

It is important to explore patients' awareness of and reactions to their own terminal illness in order to assess their need for further information or support. Research has shown that patients often know they have a serious illness, even when they have not been explicitly told. Nursing experience confirms this. We may be well aware that a patient is anxious because he suspects he has cancer. A study by McIntosh (1977) showed how patients responded differently to information about their illness. Some people wanted more information while others were content with the minimum level to enable them to cope with their situation. In McIntosh's study, 88 per cent of patients knew or suspected that they had cancer, but most of these did not want further information. McIntosh felt that those who wanted to know more would ask. However, many patients are reticent about asking medical staff or 'busy' nurses for information, unless they are given explicit opportunities to talk about their suspicions and fears. If patients are anxious and are not given explanations of their condition or treatment, they may imagine something far more frightening than the reality. They and their families may need considerable help along the road to knowledge and ultimately towards a peaceful death.

ASSESSING COPING STYLES AND
PLANNING SUPPORT

Defensiveness in the face of actual or suspected bad news is a necessary and even helpful response in patients and relatives because it helps
them to maintain a degree of hopefulness for the future and gives
patients the opportunity to take the lead in asking for information.
Total truth, presented in an uncompromising manner, can be as
damaging to patients and relatives as a conspiracy of silence by
professionals. We need to be able to identify each patient's coping
style and its possible consequences. For example, denial of the seri-
ousness of the situation may be helpful to patients in the earlier stages
of their illness because it helps them to cope with surgery or unpleasant chemotherapy. If denial continues, however, it may mean that
communication within the family becomes blocked and members are
left unsupported in their anxiety. Elizabeth Kubler Ross (1970)
describes five reactions to impending loss, i.e. denial, anger, bargaining, depression, and acceptance. I would add anxiety as being an
emotion experienced by most patients at different stages of their
terminal illness. Relatives can react to impending bereavement in a
similar way, although, as the patient's experience draws to a close, the
relatives' experience is just beginning. C. S. Lewis (1961) describes
his feelings when his wife was dying of cancer.

'I had my miseries, not hers; she had hers, not mine. The
end of hers would be the coming of age of mine. We were
setting out on different roads. This cold truth, this terrible
traffic regulation ("you, madam to the right – you, sir, to the
left") is just the beginning of the separation which is death
itself.'

The stages in coping with terminal illness, described by Kubler
Ross, can be interpreted too literally. Some patients, for example,
may appear to pass through a stage of denial to one of acceptance, but
when further signs of the advance of the disease appear, they may
deny the deterioration. There is also a danger in regarding all defences
as essentially bad when in fact they may be helping particular
individuals to cope in a time of great personal stress. It can be particularly difficult in a long illness to maintain the fine balance between
hope and reality, so that the patient does not fall into despair. For
example, it may be envisaged that a patient with motor neurone

disease will soon require a wheelchair which has been adjusted to his needs. The order for the wheelchair has to be placed considerably in advance of when it is actually needed. The difficulty for staff is in getting the patient to accept that the wheelchair will ultimately be required when his condition deteriorates, while at the same time maintaining confidence and independence in the present. Some patients reach a point in their illness when they are neither depressed nor angry with their fate. This stage of acceptance is not the same as giving up in the sense of being unable to fight any longer. Kubler Ross (1970) describes the stage of acceptance as follows:

'Acceptance should not be mistaken for a happy stage. It is almost void of feelings. It is as if the pain had gone, the struggle is over and there comes a time for "the final rest before the long journey" as one patient phrased it. It is also a time during which the family usually needs more help, understanding and support than the patient himself.'

Some of the reactions to impending loss and the implications for support of patients and relatives are now considered.

Denial – acceptance

A person who is using denial as a means of coping, discourages others from giving him information about his illness because he wishes to make his situation appear less frightening to himself. When a person's condition deteriorates it becomes more difficult to deny the reality of the situation. Patients and relatives need to talk to us openly about their fears and if we allow them to persist too long in denial, problems may not be aired and anxieties will increase. It is important to make an accurate assessment of any sources of anxiety. However, truth should be given gently and there is a need to maintain hope.

Sometimes relatives have not fully accepted the person's terminal illness although they are aware of the diagnosis. In the hospice, one man was holding on to the hope that his wife had been admitted for observation and would be going home.

'This is the place that's got the name for careful monitoring of any patient, so I was very relieved to get her in here. Are there any other patients in here for monitoring? I know that most of them are seriously ill. I thought that was all you dealt with here.'

A woman had accepted that her husband had a terminal illness, but not the very short prognosis.
'It's terrible to sort of really know but not want to know. Dave's voice started to go since last Monday and I didn't know it was the illness that was causing it. I thought "He's been talking too much". I didn't twig. I didn't realise that the pain in the back is pressure from this tumour. I thought Dave would be in here a year or two years.'

Anger

Seriously ill people and their relatives may show a lot of anger or aggression. Often this disguises underlying fears and anxieties. If a patient's anger is directed against relatives and friends or caring professionals, it may discourage them from trying to help, thus leaving the person lonely and isolated. Sometimes anger shows itself in constant complaints about treatment and care. Looked at from the patient's or relatives' perspective there sometimes seems to be good reason for the anger. Perhaps there was a delay in making a diagnosis, or treatment was extremely unpleasant and did not cure the patient. Unresolved anger may prevent the dying person and the family from using positively the time that remains to them. In the research at St Columba's Hospice, anger centred around the following areas as relatives perceived them:
1. Communication problems with hospital staff
2. Standard of care the patient received in hospital
3. Communication problems with general practitioners
4. Family relationship problems

Stedeford (1981) found that some terminally ill patients and their spouses were dissatisfied with communications they had had with their general practitioner and with hospital staff. Patients' and relatives' anger can be defused to some extent if they are able to talk freely about their experiences and difficulties, and when they feel satisfied that staff are accepting and trying to understand their feelings. The following examples illustrate this point.

Example 1

'On Tuesday', (prior to her mother's hospice admission) 'I phoned someone here. I don't know who it was. I spoke to

her and I think I poured out my heart to her. I was just so
cross with the GP. I felt better after it. Mum has really been
ill for a long time. They forgot about her in hospital and it's
really an awful story. The file was just lying in a basket. The
GP didn't visit unless we called him.'

Example 2
'I suppose they were a bit rushed in the hospital but she was
in great pain and she wanted something. She was given the
impression "Why do you need to disturb us?"'

It can be very difficult for staff to cope with anger when it is directed
at them, even when they sense that it is an outer manifestation of a
patient's fears and uncertainties. Being too defensive is probably not
very helpful. We may have to acknowledge actual shortcomings in our
care, if, for example, they occurred through shortage of staff, and
convey to the patient that we are trying to understand his difficulties.
Anger may cause problems to patients in their illness and relatives
during bereavement, if it leads them to brood over what might have
been. Relatives' anger may be expressed at professionals or even at the
deceased for leaving them to cope with life alone. Aspects of the reality
that is creating the anger should be explored and expectations about
care and treatment discussed to see to what extent they are realistic
and can be met or what alternatives are open. Physical activity can be
an effective, non-verbal means of expressing pent up emotion. An
outing, or involvement in craftwork, could provide such an outlet.

Bargaining

When they realise that their illness is terminal, some patients and their
relatives try to bargain with medical staff or with God for a cure or a
remission. Staff may find it difficult to respond positively since they
do not wish either to encourage unrealistic expectations or to destroy
patients' and relatives' hopes. This is a time when patients may seek
advice about alternative therapies or about alterations to their diet or
healing through prayer. We should not discourage patients from
exploring these areas, but help them to reach their own decisions
about what is right for them, unless we are aware that they are
embarking on a harmful course of action. Not taking decision-making

away from terminally ill patients is particularly important because they may be struggling to maintain some sort of control over their lives and are often all too conscious that their independence is slipping away.

Depression

Depression is often associated with actual or anticipated loss. Peter Speck (1978) points out that there are many kinds of loss involved in dying; loss of independence, physical attractiveness, role relationships and ultimately life itself. The significance of each loss depends, of course, on the individual concerned, but can be mitigated by the support received. Sadness that life will end does not seem to account for all the depression seen in terminally ill patients. Hinton (1972) found that depression increased with the length of the terminal illness and with the persistence of physical distress. Hockley (1983) found an association between multiple distressing symptoms and depression and this accords with my clinical experience at the Hospice. Stedeford (1981) found that anxiety or depression was usually the result of failure to cope with difficulties due to illness and treatment, a change in life style, unsatisfactory communications, or pre-existing marital and family problems. We should not, therefore, accept depression as an inevitable part of dying, but explore its causes so that we can give appropriate support. Many experienced nurses will know that peaceful and even happy deaths do occur and can leave a lasting impression on relatives, friends and staff. Spiritual and emotional difficulties are often closely linked. For example, a patient whose feelings of guilt are making him depressed may be helped by a talk with the chaplain or clergyman.

Anxiety

Most terminally ill patients and their relatives are anxious about the future and some show extreme anxiety. Patients may be anxious about frightening symptoms such as pain or dyspnoea, about becoming confused or losing control and dignity (see Chapter 4). Some patients are afraid of death and may be unable to sleep because of fears of dying at this time. Distressing symptoms can make a person feel unsafe at home and can be a reason for admission to hospice or hospital, as the following example shows.

'Soon after she was in, I saw she was more relaxed. She says
"I've still got the pain, but it's not so dreadful, and I'm not
afraid because I know people will help me."'

Patients may feel unable to cope with treatment such as chemotherapy because of its distressing side effects, yet be afraid that their
illness will progress rapidly if treatment is stopped, as the following
example illustrates.

'What frightened Margaret was the thought that it was the
end and the hospice wouldn't do anything for her. Her own
doctor said "We could take you into the hospice", but she
said "No", so they took her into the hospital and she got
more treatment there.'

Relatives are naturally anxious about the patient's daily condition
but also worry about how they will cope with the terminal illness and
with their own bereavement (see Chapter 6). The responsibility of
caring for dying people at home and ensuring, for example, that they
do not fail, can be exhausting for relatives. The cumulative effect of
being almost continuously with a sick person takes its toll, as the
following examples show.

A daughter describes caring for her mother at home.

'You're sort of worried about her all the time. Everything
just seemed to get on top of me. My sisters have been upset
and I've been upset, but I've been the one that's had to carry
them along.'

A son was anxious about the effects of his father's illness on his
mother.

'She'd rarely leave the house. Really she had 23 hours a day
with him and some very bad nights when he was restless.
Nothing too dramatic but a lot to live with all the time.'

When a dying person is living alone, this is usually a concern to
relatives even if they are living nearby, and is often a contributory
factor in hospital or hospice admission.

'My sister and I were worried especially at night. I wanted to
be there in case she was in pain. She was on her own at night
and that was the biggest worry.'

The most helpful factor in alleviating anxiety in patients and relatives is a professional who is well known and trusted and whose
judgement is respected, hence the need for early involvement of the
district nurse and/or Macmillan nurse. Patients can feel secure in

hospital or hospice, even if their distressing symptoms are not completely controlled, if they feel confident in the staff. Very anxious relatives may be helped to cope by involvement in the patient's nursing care. Nurses should take the initiative in suggesting this, when they consider that is may be helpful. Patients and relatives should be encouraged to talk about any nebulous fears they have in a more specific way. Often it is not so much the thought of death that makes patients afraid as fear of dying, or anxiety about some imagined effect of their disease, such as choking or suffocating or having uncontrolled pain. When the patient or relatives have expressed more precisely the nature of their anxieties it is often possible for the nurse to give genuine reassurance.

Dependence

Some patients become excessively dependent on professionals or family members at an early stage of their terminal illness. They may be encouraged in this by their relatives or by the nurses caring for them and may be prevented from living as positively and fully as they might if they were more independent. Relatives too can become overdependent on staff, especially when the patient's terminal illness is a long one. They come to rely on certain staff members for support and this dependence can continue into bereavement. Occupational therapists are orientated towards encouraging patients to be as independent as possible, even in small ways, even when helping them would make things easier and quicker for the staff. It is not a kindness to encourage patients even when terminally ill, to become too dependent, especially if there is a prospect of a remission or of their going home for a while.

Obsessional behaviour

Some dying patients develop a tendency to obsessional behaviour, such as noting down all the details of their treatment or tidying the contents of a bedside locker. Obsessional behaviour may be an effort on the patient's part to regain control of the situation.

LOOKING FOR CUES

It is important to be sensitive to patients' verbal and non-verbal cues in order to assess their psychological needs and to offer appropriate support. Patients may indicate in a variety of ways that they want to talk to us about their illness, treatment or other problems. Of course, we too, consciously or unconsciously, give cues to patients and relatives about our own readiness to listen. We may sometimes recognise in ourselves signs which indicate whether or not we are ready to enter into discussion with a patient. It is easy to forget that uniforms and hospitals can be intimidating and confusing and patients and relatives often rely on us to indicate that we have set time aside to talk to them.

In the research at St Columba's Hospice, relatives were generally very satisfied with their communications with nurses, but a few relatives perceived areas of difficulty in initiating communication and obtaining the information needed or support required. Adequacy of communications was not linked to the length of the patient's stay. Sometimes a relative had visited the Hospice for several days before he or she had spoken to a nurse apart from during the admission procedure. Some relatives seemed more willing to approach staff than others. Some admitted to being 'shy' and others felt that the nurses should make the approach. A few relatives commented that they would have liked a member of the nursing staff to sit and talk to them and allow them opportunities for questions.

Maguire (1975) in a study of women with breast cancer, found that nurses did not always pick up patients' verbal and non-verbal cues. If women were crying, staff did not enquire the reasons for this and therefore did not give adequate support. This research revealed a lack of opportunities for asking questions or discussing concerns.

POTENTIAL PROBLEM AREAS

There are potential problem areas in breaking the news of a terminal illness or poor prognosis to patients and relatives, namely:

1. Deciding who should tell
2. Telling the relatives
3. Explaining the meaning of symptoms
4. Coordinating communications in the professional team
5. Giving adequate follow-up support.

Deciding who should tell

The doctor is usually the person who discloses a terminal diagnosis to a patient and relatives. However, it may be the nurse who is available at the time that a patient plucks up the courage to ask about his illness. The nurse may also be the person to whom patients relate most easily, being involved in so much of their personal care. If medical and nursing colleagues work closely together, patients can be encouraged to seek information and express their anxieties without nurses becoming defensive in case they are asked awkward questions. Nurses who are prepared to listen in such a way to patients can help their medical colleagues to break the bad news of a terminal diagnosis in a sensitive way. In some instances, when no doctor is available (e.g. at night), it may be kinder for the nurse to answer a patient's questions about his illness, rather than allow an opportunity to pass.

Telling the relatives

Sometimes a wife, husband, or other relative of the patient is first told of the terminal diagnosis. Implicit in this method of telling is the assumption that the patient will not be able to cope. However, apart from the ethical considerations of whether it is right to keep such information from the patient, there are dangers in this method. Patients and relatives may be unable to support each other because of the feeling that they must protect each other from the bad news. A conspiracy of silence can isolate family members at a time when they most need to trust each other. If the relative chooses not to tell the patient, this can leave the nurse in a very difficult situation, especially if the patient is obviously seeking more information. Sometimes a situation may arise where the relative knows about, and the patient suspects, the terminal illness, but neither is able to confide in the other. Children may also be caught up in the conspiracy of silence. Opening up family communication is considered in more detail in

Chapter 5, but at the time of diagnosis, patient and relatives should, if possible, be seen together by medical and nursing staff.

Explaining the meaning of symptoms

If no adequate explanation has been given about the meaning of symptoms, this may increase patients' fears. They may become concerned about new symptoms or the implications of an obvious deterioration in their condition.

Coordinating communications in the professional team

It is important for professionals to meet regularly as a team so that communication with and support for patients and relatives are planned. A record should be kept of important communications between doctors, nurses, patients and relatives about diagnosis, prognosis or treatment. If no such record is kept, it will be difficult to secure the maximum cooperation from professional colleagues in supporting patients and relatives. Patients too will be unable to trust a team whose members seem uncertain about their situation.

Giving adequate follow-up support

Sometimes patients and relatives are told that a terminal illness has been diagnosed but thereafter are given little support by staff. General practitioners in the community may be unsure of what the patient has been told. As a result, communication can break down and valuable time is lost while decisions are delayed. When a terminally ill patient has been discharged from hospital, follow-up clinic appointments can cause more stress than benefit if it is obvious to the patient that the staff feel there is nothing more they can offer. If a district nurse or Macmillan nurse attends the clinic with the patient, she may be able to prompt the patient to ask about those things which are causing difficulties and thus make the visit worthwhile. Hospital nurses could do more to help such patients by taking time to explore with them any difficulties they are having at home, before they see the doctor.

Several studies have demonstrated the effectiveness of counselling in reducing stress in patients with cancer. For example, Maguire (1975) found that where counselling occurred before and after operations for cancer of the breast, psychological distress was reduced. Patients and relatives should be encouraged to ask questions and express their anxieties when a serious illness is suspected, when it has been diagnosed and in the period following the diagnosis. Many of us will have had the experience of trying to help a relative or friend to cope with a serious illness and will be aware that he or she needed to talk to us often about feelings and difficulties and treatment options. There is a need for more nurses to develop counselling skills to maximise the support that they can give to patients in the limited time available.

In this chapter, I have tried to demonstrate that breaking bad news about a terminal illness demands skills in listening, observation, and empathy, as much as the ability to choose the right words. It is important to be aware of how much the dying person knows and how much he wishes to know about his illness. There are no rules about when, how and what to tell, as each person must be treated individually. A team approach to talking with dying people is important, as each person should be able to seek information and help at the time he chooses. His confidence in the professional team will depend on all its members being sensitive and open in their communication with him.

Questions and exercises

1. How do you assess whether dying patients and their relatives are coping emotionally?
2. Which of the following emotions do you find most difficult to respond to in dying patients and their relatives?
   Denial
   Anger
   Bargaining
   Depression
   Anxiety
   Why is this so?
3. Consider how best you could plan support for patients or relatives expressing the above emotions.
4. How well do you and your professional colleagues work as a team in communicating with the terminally ill? What do you do well? How could you make further improvements?

Assessing continuing 4
needs for information
and support

In my experience the assessment of patients' and relatives' needs for
information requires great sensitivity and skill from nurses, not only
at the time of diagnosis, but in the following weeks or months of the
terminal illness. As indicated in Chapter 3, awareness of a terminal
illness does not always mean acceptance of its implications. Many
people fear dying rather than death, imagining that they will have
pain or other distressing symptoms and fearing that the doctors and
nurses will be able to do little to help them. Relatives feel some
degree of responsibility if a dying person is obviously suffering, and
especially if they are caring for him at home. As nurses, we should
help people to explore and express their anxieties, so that we can give
appropriate explanations and support. In my experience, nurses can
usually give genuine reassurance that dying will not be as distressing
as they may imagine.

People who are terminally ill often have several distressing
symptoms which may cause anxiety or embarrassment to themselves
and their relatives. Symptoms such as dyspnoea or pain may be
frightening, while incontinence or a fungating wound can be
embarrassing. When staff take time to listen to such anxieties and to
give explanations, much reassurance can be given. As one relative
observed:

'The cancer went from the chest and lung up to the head. I
visualised terrible things when it went to the head. The
doctor explained what would happen. It made me feel
better.'

It is important to try to find out how much patients and relatives
wish to know about the illness or treatment so that information is
given when requested and needed. Some people will want more
information than others, and their needs will vary at different stages
of the illness.

32

UNDERSTANDING FEARS

Two of four areas of difficulty identified by Stedeford (1981) for terminally ill patients and their relatives, were coping with direct effects of the illness and its treatment and inadequate communications both within the family and between patients, relatives, and professionals.

'Patients regarded general practitioners and hospital staff as erring on the side of saying far too little or else imparting information in an abrupt and blunt fashion.'

The issue of whether or not to continue with treatment was raised by six couples in Stedeford's study, but the fear of uncontrolled pain was not a major concern because it was successfully controlled. Fears about insanity and loss of control were fairly common. Woodhall (1986) found that peoples' attitudes towards their illness and its symptoms seemed to be important in determining whether they stayed at home or were admitted to St Christopher's Hospice. Of home patients, 90 per cent had mainly positive emotional responses to their illness in comparison with 63 per cent of patients who were admitted to the Hospice. This illustrates the importance of allowing people to express their anxieties and to receive emotional support at home.

In my own research, all the patients admitted to St Columba's Hospice had undergone some physical deterioration prior to admission, and most had several distressing symptoms, with pain, immobility, and/or falls being most frequently mentioned, followed by nausea/vomiting, dyspnoea and confusion. These symptoms were frightening for many patients and their effects are now examined in more detail.

Pain

Where poorly controlled pain has been present, patients and relatives usually have distressing memories. Patients' experiences of pain should be explored and their anxieties respected, so that they are encouraged to report pain rather than suffer in silence. The following example illustrates the potentially devastating effects of uncontrolled pain.

'He's been ill for more than a year. He didn't get any strong painkillers at home. He was in agony, pain all the time. If

he'd known what he was going to suffer, he'd have
committed suicide. He couldn't get anywhere to put himself
to be at rest.'

Immobility and falls

Relatives often report their fear that a patient may fall. The fear of falls
is a particular worry when the patient is living alone, or when an
elderly relative is not strong enough to cope with the consequences of
a fall.

'My Dad got so heavy and so difficult to move that my Mum
just couldn't cope with him. She couldn't sleep having to be
alert to his needs and she couldn't move him readily through
to the toilet. She just cracked up. If he fell, she couldn't get
him up again.'

Relatives' own assessment of how they are coping with the care of
terminally ill patients should be explored and their perceived
limitations respected.

Vomiting and nausea

It is worrying for relatives if a patient is unable to keep any food down,
despite efforts to tempt him or her to eat. Also, constant nausea and
vomiting leave a person feeling miserable. Patients and relatives need
help on how to cope with this. They can be advised, for example, to
serve small frequent snacks rather than large meals at set times. The
following examples illustrate the problems patients and relatives can
encounter:

Example 1
'In the last five or six weeks, it's been awful. The sickness
hasn't eased. She really did deteriorate rapidly over the last
few days. She felt so awful, she'd have gone anywhere, done
anything.'

Example 2
'The main problem was the nausea all the time. She was sick
during the night. If she saw a tray with a knife and fork,
she'd be sick. My Mum's not been eating through the nausea

and she couldn't take her anti-nausea medicine. That was coming up as well. It was like a vicious circle.'

Dyspnoea

Dyspnoea is perhaps the most frightening symptom for both patients and relatives. Often there seems little that relatives can do to help and their anxiety is conveyed to the patient, thus exacerbating the situation. Dyspnoea is particularly frightening for carers and patients to cope with at home. Relatives describe feeling helpless as the patient struggles for breath.

Example 1
'My husband's cough has been terrible. Talk about being frightened. It's as if he's going to choke. You can't do anything because you can't breathe for a person which is what you want.'

An elderly man was living alone and his son describes how his father would wake up at night, fighting for breath.

Example 2
'He was lonely, but he was more frightened because of his breathlessness. He would wake up at night and he had an attack. He couldn't breathe and there was nobody to help him.'

The perceived availability of medical and nursing staff seems to give many of these dyspnoeic patients a sense of security.

Confusion

Confusion is difficult to cope with and sometimes causes acute embarrassment to relatives. It is considered in more detail in Chapter 5.

EXPECTATIONS ABOUT TREATMENT
AND SYMPTOM CONTROL

Patients and relatives feel more relaxed even when symptoms are not greatly alleviated, if nurses are perceived to be available and confident in their approach. The non-verbal reassurance patients and relatives can experience through the presence of experienced and attentive staff is as important as anything doctors or nurses may say to them. Hampe (1985) found that the patients' comfort was one of the most important factors in meeting relatives' needs.

In my own research, most relatives were satisfied that the patient was being kept comfortable and that symptoms had been alleviated, if not fully controlled. Patients' attitudes seemed to influence relatives' perceptions of the effectiveness of symptom control. If patients were content, the relatives were also happy with the level of care. Relatives' expectations of symptom control in the Hospice were realistic, major concerns being the comfort and contentment of the patient, rather than any dramatic improvement in his or her condition. One relative expressed the sentiments of many in this regard.

'I'm glad she's not suffering. She's comfortable. She's in
people's hands who know what they are doing. She's getting
her meals.'

Another relative recognised that her husband's condition was deteriorating, but was pleased that he seemed more comfortable and was able to enjoy his food again.

'Although he's gone down and down, I feel he's gone down
and down in comfort, getting the medication right, the
timing. He's eating more food here. He's enjoying his food. I
think it's that he's with people who have got experience and
that's what they want at this stage of their illness. They want
to live as long as they can, so they want to know they're in
the right hands.'

Sometimes relatives express a definite wish for palliative care in contrast to more active forms of treatment which they felt were no longer benefitting the patient. One relative felt that her mother's condition should not be subjected to further investigation.

'In hospital they said they were going to do body scans. I
just wanted her here where she could get looked after
properly.'

Relatives perceived some symptoms to be more successfully controlled than others, but most were alleviated to some degree. For example, pain was completely controlled or greatly alleviated in most cases and dyspnoea was alleviated in over half the cases. Several patients mentioned feeling secure although their symptoms had not always been completely controlled as the following examples show:

Example 1
'He knows if he coughs and gets into that terrible state, someone is there helping him. He knows he's safe.'

Example 2
'His biggest fear and worry was being on his own. He couldn't breathe. It's just the psychological effect here of knowing there's someone there to help him. He feels happy and he feels secure.'

Sometimes when symptoms are alleviated, patient or relatives seem almost to forget about the distress they caused.
'As far as I know, the vomiting has stopped and the pain has stopped too. She doesn't complain about them, so I presume they're not there.'

MATCHING SUPPORT TO THE NEED

As nurses we should be alert to situations where patients and relatives may be anxious and we should be prepared to give explanations about the effects of drugs the patient is receiving, procedures being carried out or about the appearance of new symptoms. In my research, patients and relatives seemed to want more information about the illness, symptoms or treatment when they were anxious about some aspects of this. Four relatives wanted to know more about the drugs the patient was receiving, and five about the effects of the illness. One patient had obviously been afraid of the implications of starting on morphine when at home. The following examples illustrate how easily misunderstandings can arise.

Example 1

'He was trying to conceal his pain from everyone. He was maybe trying to prolong the time before he started on morphine because, let's face it, when you start on morphine, you know you are critically ill. Everyone knows that morphine is for when you're critically ill, when you're very much in pain. I thought morphine was going to make him a bit dozy, but it didn't do anything to the brain. I had it wrong. They're still just as intelligent and alert.'

Example 2

'I spoke to Dr Douglas because my sister was worried by the fact that she was dopey, so much under the influence of drugs. Dr Douglas said she would reduce the dose which I think she's done, without allowing the pain to intrude again.'

Example 3

'I knew he was on diamorphine at home. I was worried about it, especially with a teenager at home. You can't have big bottles of diamorphine in the house.'

One man felt ambivalent about the prospect of his wife's discharge from the hospice because of his fears about a new symptom and how he could cope.

Example 4

'She's got a new symptom now with this brachial plexus thing. I'm afraid of her becoming more paralysed. I hope it never happens. I think I'm going to have her home again. I don't know whether I'm strong enough. I wonder if it's even fair to expect that?'

RELATIVES' NEEDS

Wright and Dyck (1984) explored the needs of cancer patients and their families. In this American study, the most frequently cited primary concerns related to dealing with symptoms, fear of the future, waiting and trying to obtain information. Relatives' highest priorities were to be kept informed of a patient's condition and to be assured that he or she was comfortable. Families of patients who were experiencing a recurrence of their cancer scored significantly higher on a 'need scale' than families at the time of diagnosis or during the terminal phase of the illness. Wright and Dyck (1984) comment as follows:

'At this stage, families realise that the much hoped-for cure has not occurred and doctors and patients reach a communication impasse, thus isolating patients (and families) from the health care team and increasing their anxiety.'

Relatives had difficulty eliciting concrete answers from doctors, contacting doctors, getting information by telephone or finding out about the patient's daily progress from the nurses. Wright and Dyck comment on the prime position of nurses in easing emotional stress for patients and relatives.

'Families expect the nurses to explain daily procedures, treatments, medications and their possible side effects. This type of information is viewed as being helpful in terms of families being able to cope more realistically with the immediate future. The worry that accompanies waiting cannot always be eliminated.'

In my own research, most relatives did not want detailed information about drugs, treatment or the patient's illness if the patient seemed comfortable. This echoes Wright and Dyck's (1984) findings for relatives' needs in the terminal phase of a patient's illness. In St Columba's Hospice, updating on the patient's overall condition was viewed as very important. Many relatives preferred to cope with their anxieties on a day-to-day basis, meeting difficulties as they arose. Two relatives explicitly mentioned feeling less need for information about the patient's illness and treatment than they did when they were in hospital because they knew that the illness was terminal, but also because they were confident that the patient would be kept comfortable.

Example 1

'I don't know what she's on. She's on injections every four hours, so I assume it's diamorphine. I know less than the staff know, but I know enough for myself. I know the state of affairs. If she were deteriorating a lot, they would ask to speak to me.'

Example 2
'I could speak to the doctors but they can't tell me any
different from what I already know. I take it day by day. I
use my own judgement when I see Jeanie.'

GIVING SENSITIVE SUPPORT

Many writers have stressed the role of explanations and psychological
support in alleviating patients' and relatives' anxieties about the
effects of a terminal illness and its treatment. Such support is as

essential as the medical treatment itself. It is easy for doctors and nurses to forget that patients and relatives may be worrying unnecessarily about the effects of drugs such as diamorphine, or that they may fear the imagined consequences of the spread of the disease to other parts of the body. It is equally easy for doctors and nurses to overlook the extent to which patients can naturally give support to each other, since they are often best placed to empathise with someone in a similar situation to their own. Skilled support involves giving information when it is perceived to be needed by patients or relatives and being alert to situations when patients and relatives may be anxious. Too much information may provoke as much anxiety as too little, and it should always be tailored to the individual's needs.

In this chapter, I have explored some of the fears and anxieties of dying patients and their relatives. Their emotional responses to terminal illness can determine whether they live actively and positively, maintaining a hopeful outlook, or whether they are consumed by fear of what is happening to them or have anxieties about the future. The alleviation of physical distress does not depend exclusively on giving skilled physical care. It also depends on understanding and helping dying people with their fears. It is inevitable that patients and relatives will experience varying degrees of anxiety at the time a terminal illness is diagnosed, when there are signs of recurrence, or when it appears that a terminal phase has been reached. Our role should be to alleviate their fears by giving appropriate information and support and by the assurance that we will meet any problems together. Dying people and their relatives need to know that we are as interested and skilled in their palliative care as we were when there was a possibility of cure.

Questions and exercises

1. How do you ensure that relatives are updated on a dying patient's daily condition? Should you take more initiative in this area?
2. In what ways do you try to elicit patients' and relatives' knowledge and anxieties about the symptoms or treatment of a terminal condition?
3. Think about the last time a dying patient in your care expressed an anxiety about his illness or treatment. What was his problem? How

did you reassure him? In what ways do you think you succeeded? What more could you have done?

4. What fears, if any, have terminally ill patients and their relatives expressed to you about the use of such drugs as morphine or diamorphine? How have you reassured them about this?

5. It can be difficult to support patients and relatives when there has been a recurrence of the disease or a deterioration in the patient's condition. How do you support them at this time? In what ways is your support most effective? In what ways could your support for them be improved?

Planning support for   5
family and close friends

When a person with a potentially serious condition is being cared for in hospital, the needs of the family for information and support can often seem a lesser priority than making an early diagnosis and starting to treat the illness. Nurses are often in daily contact with relatives when they visit a person in hospital and are in a good position to be aware of their needs. In planning nursing support, it is important that the needs of the terminally ill person and his relatives and close friends are considered together. I have found that when family members are unable or afraid to share their feelings with each other much distress can arise. Relatives and patients can give each other mutual comfort and support if they are able to talk to each other openly and are not trying to protect each other by concealing their anxieties. I include children in the term relatives because they suffer when a loved parent or relative is ill and can sometimes be excluded from the support professionals give to adult family members.

IDENTIFYING THOSE NEEDING SUPPORT

As nurses we should try to identify all the patient's family members, including children, at an early stage. Close friends of the patient should also be noted to ensure that no one is isolated from communication and support. This can happen when we communicate only with the next of kin. If one relative is being interviewed initially, we should ask if there are others with whom we should talk. A family tree diagram may be helpful in ensuring that a more complete picture is obtained. An example is given below.

FAMILY AWARENESS AND COMMUNICATION

Glaser and Strauss (1965) noted that 'open awareness' and discussion of the terminal illness eased communication for staff, patient and family, while 'closed awareness' increased their difficulties. Open awareness is a situation in which each person feels free to discuss matters of concern with others.

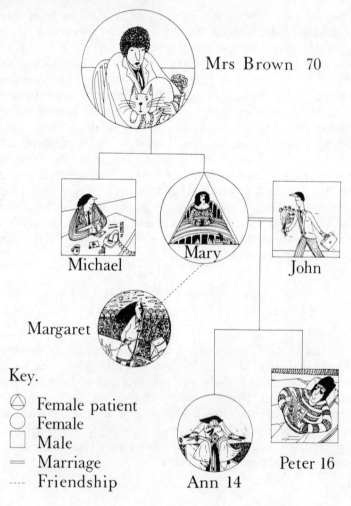

Mrs Brown 70

Michael

Mary

John

Margaret

Key.

⊖ Female patient
◯ Female
▢ Male
= Marriage
---- Friendship

Ann 14

Peter 16

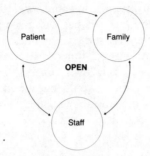

Where communication is 'closed', communication barriers exist. Stedeford (1981) 'in a study of dying patients and their spouses' notes:

'In instances where blocked communications with husband and wife coexist with severe depression or anxiety in the patient, these symptoms are often relieved when the pair can be helped to be more open with each other.'

My hospice research revealed that interactions between patients and their relatives ranged along a continuum from completely open to closed. Confused patients and children were more difficult to place on this continuum. Most relatives and patients were aware of the terminal nature of the patient's condition, but the extent to which this was discussed in the family varied. In seven families, there were communication problems because the patient was confused or too ill to talk. In nine families, communication between patient and relatives was poor for other reasons e.g. the patient's anxiety and unwillingness to talk or patients' and relatives' desire to protect each other from painful awareness of the short time they would have together. We should not assume, therefore, that because both patients and relatives know the diagnosis, the implications of this knowledge have been discussed or that they have been able to share their feelings.

Open awareness

My research revealed that most families had discussed the diagnosis frankly and had considered the implications for the future of their surviving family members. Some relatives had taken on new roles, since the patient's illness, for example, housekeeping or driving the car. It was very helpful to both patients and relatives to be able to discuss together their progress in coping with those changes.

Several patients and relatives had discussed the possibility of the relative moving house after the patient's death. A few patients and relatives had even discussed funeral arrangements. Three male patients had arranged their own funerals and one couple had discussed where the patient would be buried. The ability to talk together and express their feelings seemed helpful to both patients and relatives. One son said:

Example 1
'My dad's aware of what's wrong. We have no problems discussing things frankly. I mean, he wants to know. He said "You find out and tell me" and I've told him absolutely everything.'

Example 2
'We've talked the whole thing through, my wife and I. We spoke about the end. We said "We've had a good life. We're 72. Aren't we lucky?"'

Closed awareness

Sometimes patients are unable to express their fears and anxieties about dying to their relatives. Relatives find this situation difficult and are often unsure of how to resolve matters, as the following examples show. The wife of one patient said:

Example 1
'I was speaking to Sister Alice. She said she thought he was a very frightened man which he is. He's been like this because they told him this would be his last winter. I've been frightened myself to approach him because I don't know how he's going to take it from me.'

One young man, recently bereaved, had wanted the hospice staff to help him talk to his father.

Example 2
'I'm sure he knew he had cancer, but it was something he never mentioned. I would have liked to have talked to him

and perhaps even had a member of staff there for his own
peace of mind. I think he knew he was dying anyway. I felt
there was a barrier there. That's my one regret, that there
wasn't enough talking.'

In fact, the hospice doctor had encouraged the patient and his wife
to talk more openly to each other prior to hospice admission, but this
openness had obviously not extended to the son.

Opening up communications within the family

Communications within the family may be helped if a nurse speaks to
the family together, encouraging each member to express his or her
feelings. Families use different methods to resolve their problems.
Sometimes these are dealt with openly, or they may be only partly
solved, leaving unresolved feelings. If there have been difficulties in
relationships, there may be feelings of guilt which need to be talked
about openly. Sometimes conflicts cannot be resolved, but patients
and relatives still need support. In every family, some role-taking is
inevitable, but sometimes roles are so fixed that change is difficult. It
is important to talk to patients and relatives directly, either as
individuals or as a family, as well as talking about them with
colleagues. This will help to avoid 'labelling' patients and relatives as,
for example, 'difficult', or reinforcing unhelpful patterns of interaction within the family.

The patients' and relatives' pace in coming to terms with their
situation has to be respected by staff who are giving support, and it
should be recognised that patients and relatives may be at different
stages in their grieving. Relatives and patients expect, rightly, that
while open and honest communication will be encouraged, this will be
done in a sensitive way.

In my research, one elderly couple had been very anxious when the
husband was a home care patient. On admission, a hospice doctor
encouraged more open communication between them by talking to
them together. The patient's wife describes this meeting.

'The doctor said: "Do you ever talk to your husband about
these things?" I said "Well, sometimes I do." He said "I
want you to tell your husband everything. You're both
married. You both know all about each other. You're
worried about him. He's worrying about you. If there's

anything at all, you speak to your husband about it and your
husband will speak to you. You'll get relief by talking about
it." It's true. It helps, because we were frightened to say
anything to each other at first.'

Obviously, acceptance of a harsh reality is more difficult for some
people than for others. A few relatives openly express a wish not to be
told about a patient's prognosis and prefer to take each day as it
comes.

CONFUSED PATIENTS

Relatives often have difficulties in communicating with confused
patients. Confusion sometimes causes embarrassment to relatives
who find it difficult to relate to someone with whom they can no longer
communicate. One hospice patient had a brain tumour and his wife
had been embarrassed on several occasions by his behaviour whilst at
home.

   Example 1
   'He was hyperactive. He was getting lost and being brought
   back by the police. His mental condition went down. He
   couldn't eat properly, see properly. His memory was so bad.
   We had one or two outbursts when we were at the shops.'

The daughter of the man described above was very upset because in
her last conversation with him, her father had told her to 'Go away'.
Shortly after his admission to the hospice, he became unconscious, so
she felt that she had been unable to say good-bye to him. Some
confused patients had little insight into what was happening to them.

   Example 2
   'She has been told. It seems to be a mental block. Not long
   ago, when she was beginning to get really bad, she said
   "What was it the doctor said was wrong with me?" She's a
   bit confused and there's lots of things she isn't taking in.'

A young woman worried about how nurses would react to her
mother who was a little confused and seemed unhappy.

Example 3

'I think the staff are seeing her as not a very nice person,
whereas I know that in her true self, she's not really like
what she is now. I feel that makes them not like her as much
as I would like them to like her. I spoke to one of the staff
nurses. She was very concerned and she was well aware that
she's not always been like that.'

Supporting relatives of confused patients

Developing understanding in the care of the confused patient is
important, since it is often the relatives who suffer most in this
situation. We can help relatives with the stigma of having a family
member who is confused by demonstrating that the person has not
lost all dignity or right to respect and by trying to learn from the
relatives what the person was like before he or she became confused.
Stedeford (1981) found that mildly confused patients responded with
great relief to reassurance such as 'Whatever odd things your brain
tumour makes you say or do, I still know that you, yourself, are all
right.' This enabled people to distinguish between concepts of
'myself' and 'my illness'.

Clear signals can keep confused people orientated towards reality.
For instance, good lighting, a clock at the bedside, siting the bed near
the toilet or near the window and having a daily routine, are all
helpful, especially when the person is in unfamiliar surroundings. We
should encourage confused patients to talk about their fears which
may sometimes aggravate confusion, and show relatives the value of
non-verbal communication in showing love and concern to the
confused person. Sometimes in hospital, relatives are afraid to touch
the patient or to take the 'cot sides' down unless they are encouraged
to do so. Familiar items such as family photographs may encourage
the confused person to remember important family events, and also
give relatives the opportunity to talk to staff about the patient's past
life, thus removing some of the stigma of confusion and revealing the
'real' person behind the present condition. Sometimes the confused
person's memory for past events is quite good, even when the
short-term memory is poor. The relative quoted earlier whose
husband had a cerebral tumour, commented on his obvious enjoy-
ment of visits to the day hospice despite his failing memory.

'He had three visits to the day centre. He'd met other people and he's met someone who had been in India sometime and had a chin wag because he remembered things from long ago. But even things from long ago are getting a bit muddled up.'

COMMUNICATING WITH CHILDREN

Children need particularly sensitive understanding to help them cope with impending bereavement, and their awareness of the terminal illness and needs for support should be explored and determined. Raphael (1984) noted that a child's response to death should be viewed in a family context. Parental attitudes to death, openness with children and the support they receive from the extended family can be an important influence on children's attitudes. Stedeford (1981) noted that many couples did not talk to their children about the terminal illness until the children asked questions. In my own research, communication between adult members and children seemed to be fairly open, possibly because most children in the study were losing a grandparent and not a parent. Experience at St Columba's Hospice has shown that problems may arise in their bereavement if children are not involved when a close relative is terminally ill. None of the 26 children involved in my study were interviewed, so the views attributed to them are those of their parents or grandparents.

Children's age and understanding of death

Children's understanding of death varies with age but honest explanations and allowing children to talk about their feelings are important regardless of age. Younger children may be unable to understand the permanence of death and may think that a parent, who has died, will return. Jobling (1975), summarising research findings into bereavement among children, wrote:
'Very young children have limited comprehension but seeing death as separation, may react with profound grief. While pre-school children may be bewildered or may appear callously to ignore death, this is a time when parents are most needed as identification models. . . . Five to eight year

olds are in the stage of 'magical thinking', believing that
wishing can make something come true. . . . They often
become especially good and conscientious, as if in hope of
restoring the dead. At about nine, children express sorrow as
adults do – they may be apathetic, withdrawn, cry a great
deal or become hostile and angry.'

Difficulties in coping with a parent or grandparent's terminal
illness are not always related to age, as older children are sometimes
more withdrawn and uncommunicative than their younger siblings.
The following hospice examples illustrate this point:

A four year old girl knew that her mother was going to die and
wanted to talk about it to her father.

Example 1
'Ann knows her mum's dying. She said "Mummy's going to
God, isn't she?" I said "Yes". She's only four and a half. It's
no use telling the bairn lies, saying her mum will be away
and she'll be back. I'm just preparing her in a nice way.
She'll never forget her mother, but she's young. She's got
her own life to lead.'

Example 2
'My own kids have seen him throughout. I think my son
may be reacting in some way. He's twelve and my daughter's
nine. My son doesn't say terribly much. My wife was talking
to him and my son was saying he didn't know what to say to
grandpa. There have been too many other people there.
We've talked to them about the whole thing.'

One teenager was afraid of being in the house when her grand-
mother died.

Example 3
'My youngest daugher (16) was frightened of her grand-
mother dying in the house. She said "If anyone died in this
house, I would have to move". Before my mother got too
bad, she was in the house with her. She was off school. She
said "I'm frightened nanny dies when I'm here". I've said to
her "That isn't likely to happen because with the illness she's
got, they gradually get worse and you know a long time
beforehand".'

As nurses we may not always adequately consider the needs of the mentally handicapped who suffer bereavement. One patient had a mentally handicapped son in hospital and had been visiting him faithfully three times a week before she became ill. Her daughter was going to take over this responsibility from her mother but had found it impossible to explain to him about his mother's illness.

'I have a young brother in hospital. He's a mongol and he doesn't speak. He's quite low grade so I can't even explain to him about her. It's quite sad really. Mum's stopped speaking about him. I don't know if it's all going over her head now or whether she realises she can't go now anyway.'

Strachan (1981) studied bereavement reactions among adult mentally handicapped residents, and found that, for long-term residents, more marked responses were often reported by nurses to deaths of other residents on the ward than for those of close relatives. Few of the handicapped were able to maintain contact in the terminal stages of their relative's illness, news of the death being broken in most cases by ward staff after they had been informed by telephone. Strachan recommends that ward staff should arrange a visit to the sick relative at home, hospital or hospice and that, whenever possible, a family member should break the news to a hospital resident. The handicapped person's need to participate in the funeral may be important even if understanding is limited.

Visiting

Sometimes children are discouraged from visiting because relatives feel that it would be a strain or an embarrassment for the dying patient or because they feel that the children could be upset by what they may see. Patients' attitudes to children's visits are also important. A few hospice patients do not want their children or grandchildren to visit them when their condition deteriorates. While patients' and relatives' wishes must be respected, they may appreciate an opportunity to discuss their feelings with a nurse. For example, one boy was helped to cope with his father's impending death by witnessing the peaceful death of another patient on the ward.

Supporting children

We should take time to speak to children and teenagers individually, as well as to adult family members. As with adults, it would be helpful for one or two nurses to introduce themselves by name. There are occasions when parents would appreciate the opportunity to talk to nurses about a child who is withdrawn or seems anxious, or to seek advice about whether a child should continue to visit when the patient's condition deteriorates.

In the hospice, several relatives wanted to talk to staff about what to say to children. This is a sensitive area, but nurses may be able to support younger children by just talking to their parents or grandparents and encouraging openness within the family. Teenagers in particular may appreciate talking to a nurse or doctor alone. Facilities such as a coffee lounge, a play area, or crèche may help children to feel more at home when visiting a relative in hospital. Fostering an attitude among nursing staff that recognises the distinctive relationships that exist between *each* member of the family and the patient, should be a key objective of the nursing approach.

In this chapter I have tried to show that the needs of dying people and their relatives are interrelated. We should be aware of all family members and close friends of each patient and of any difficulties they may be experiencing in talking openly to each other. It may be helpful, on occasions, to talk to patient and relatives together, encouraging them to share any anxieties and perhaps to demonstrate more explicitly their concern for each other. It should not be assumed that the preparation of children for bereavement should always be left to their parents and grandparents, or that this is what the latter would wish. In my experience, families of terminally ill patients are often very grateful for the assistance of a professional person, doctor or nurse who understands that they have needs distinct from those of the patient and who does not make them feel selfish in expressing those needs.

Questions and exercises

1. What steps do you take to identify all close relatives and friends of a terminally ill patient who may need support?
2. Do you try to identify the principal carer? In what ways can you give additional emotional support to the principal carer?

3. A case is quoted in this chapter where a son wanted a nurse's help in opening up communication between himself and his father. How would you have tried to help them?
4. How do you support children and adolescents who are relatives of a dying person? What do you do well? What aspects of your support could be improved?
5. Are you usually aware when communication barriers exist within families? How do you identify these barriers? When they seem too strong to be broken down, how then should the situation be managed?
6. How do you support the relatives of a confused, dying person?

Preparing relatives for bereavement   6

Relatives' preparation for bereavement begins in the preceding weeks or months of the person's terminal illness and not at the time of death. This period of preparation also provides an opportunity for nursing staff to support and counsel relatives. We can encourage them to express feelings and fears and keep them fully informed of any changes in the patient's condition. There may be opportunities to encourage family members to be more open with each other and to listen to their anxieties about the future.

In a sense, everything that is done for the patient and relatives prior to death is part of the preparation for bereavement. Relatives will probably remember any special consideration shown to them by staff and whether the person was comfortable and peaceful in the last days. On the other hand, any perceived neglect on the part of staff will also be remembered and perhaps magnified beyond its original significance.

Worden (1984) describes four tasks which mourning seems to fulfil:

1. To accept the reality of the loss
2. To experience the pain of grief
3. To adjust to an environment in which the deceased is missing
4. To withdraw emotional energy and invest it in another relationship.

The ways in which people may be helped in the first three of these tasks are now considered.

ACCEPTING THE REALITY OF IMPENDING LOSS

In the hospice, most relatives are fully aware of the terminal nature of the person's illness, but their degree of acceptance of the impending loss varies. Some relatives do not fully accept the implications of terminal illness, although they are aware of the diagnosis.

'I spent my time keeping my spirits high and refusing to listen to people. I felt I was fighting them by always sounding
hopeful, but we'd had so many disappointments. I've read all
the literature and wept for miracles. All this time I've been
indulging in prayer and all kinds of healing things and
applying my strength to telling this ruddy thing to push off.'

It is is helpful if the relatives' and patients' awareness of the diagnosis is marked in the case notes. Understanding is, however, at two
levels, intellectual and emotional. Relatives who are aware of the
diagnosis may not accept all its implications; for example, the prognosis or the advent of new symptoms. These should be pointed out
gently to them by staff as each problem arises or change occurs. In my
experience, most relatives do not wish to look too far ahead and prefer
to ask for and receive information on a day-to-day basis. In trying to
accept their impending bereavement, many relatives become anxious
and some express extreme anxiety as the following example illustrates.

'I'm just terrified. I know my husband used to go away when
he was at sea, but I knew he was there. I could always talk
to him when he came home. I don't know how I'll cope. I
was sitting in the coffee lounge and I felt I just couldn't
move. I felt as if I was rooted to the spot. I knew I'd got to
get home but I couldn't get a bus. I ordered a taxi in the
end.'

Sometimes very anxious relatives are helped to cope with their
anxiety by involvement in the patient's nursing care. There are many
simple tasks which they can easily perform – washing, feeding and
combing the patient's hair. Relatives may benefit from such involvement so long as they feel the decision to act in this way is theirs. Home
commitments, fatigue, and the wishes of the patient may mean that
some relatives do not or cannot become very involved in even simple
nursing.

EXPERIENCING THE PAIN OF GRIEF

In my hospice research, most relatives had begun to think of the
future without the dying person and some had begun to make some

sort of plans. Several relatives talked about feelings of loneliness.
Many relatives wanted to express their feelings and talk about family
problems or other difficulties they had faced or were still experiencing. Hampe (1975) found that relatives of terminally ill people
needed opportunities to ventilate their own emotions and to receive
support from family members and health professionals. We should
therefore plan our support of relatives so that we make a point of
letting them know that we care about these anxieties and that we
understand their feelings. If possible, they should be taken some-
where private and be given the opportunity to talk and ask questions
of however simple a nature. If relatives successfully try to suppress
their feelings too much, family and professionals can assume too easily
that they are coping well and do not need further support. This can
give rise to real difficulties as shown in the following quotation from
an elderly man.

'It's something I've never done before is wept at anything,
but I'm afraid this has been a bit of a shaker. The tears come
so easily and I feel so stupid about it, you know. My own
doctor said "You can let it come because you've held it in
too long." I said "I've never cracked before." This is
something which in our generation they didn't do. I believe
they do it more now. It's a release you know.'

When a patient dies in a hospice a nurse usually spends a little time
talking to bereaved relatives about the formalities of registering the
death and about funeral arrangements. There is also an opportunity to
comfort the relatives and to talk about how they are feeling or may feel
in the future.

One young man who had been bereaved when his father died in St
Columba's Hospice, had found his talk with a hospice sister very
helpful.

'The help before and after my father's death was very good.
The fact that the sister took my sister and me through to one
of the rooms and had a nice chat to us. It calmed us down
for the trauma of going home and trying to explain it to the
rest of the family.'

When encouraging relatives to talk about their future, we can
discourage them from making hasty decisions based on their present
feelings and which they might regret later. For example, some relatives consider moving house because their home is too big or has too

many memories of their (soon to be lost) loved one. They may not have explored the implications of moving away from friends and neighbours whom they have known for years and who would be well placed to give them support. Many bereaved people will be living alone for the first time. In the hospice research most seemed well supported by family and friends; seven relatives were considering moving house and five of those were living alone. An elderly man interviewed during bereavement was concerned about his sister who was living alone.

'She left her sister very comfortable in a lovely home, but I
think we may get her down beside us. She'd be better down
beside us.'

A relative of another patient had been ill herself.

'I can't stay on my own. I will go south to my son. I did
wonder about staying here on my own but I can't. I never
know when I'll be paralytic with chest pain.'

One woman was going to discuss her options with friends who had themselves been bereaved.

'In the first place, I'm doing nothing for a while, but I think
I'll have to get a smaller flat because this house has four bed-
rooms. What I would like is to see friends around the country and stay with them, one or two widows and discuss it
with them and see what they did and then decide where to
live.'

One elderly man rejected the idea of living with his son after his wife's death.

'I've looked at everything fairly carefully during this period
when my wife's been told it was terminal. I've thought
things through fairly well. I'm still living at home and I have
my meals with my son, but I prefer to go home to my own
bed. I'll just have to adjust, you see. I have a garden. I'm
one of those fortunate people whose work was his hobby.
Apart from the war years, I've worked in gardens all my
life.'

Where new roles have to be learned, it can be a great help to both patient and relatives if a beginning is made before the patient dies. Some male relatives, for example, have to learn to cook and do their own housework for the first time. Female relatives may have to learn how to cope with financial matters or learn to drive. A few people may fail to adapt or patients may resent partners taking on roles they had previously enjoyed. It is helpful for relatives to discuss and rehearse how they might cope with radical changes in life style. One elderly man had been talking to his terminally ill wife in the hospice about his management of the housekeeping and had been helped by her encouragement and that of his sister-in-law.

'It's very quiet in the house just now, on my own. I just couldn't understand what had happened to me, walking into an empty house and starting to do things for myself. We've no family and we're more or less always together. I was very, very shocked. Mattie's a bit more settled now. Her sister has been up and said "He's fairly doing well in the house. He's got it in good condition." That cheers her up.'

It is not only learning new roles that is difficult, but adapting to the loss of close companionship, shared ideas, interests, humour and even disagreements.

IDENTIFYING RELATIVES NEEDING EXTRA SUPPORT

Raphael (1984) noted that certain groups of people seemed more at risk of having difficulties during bereavement. She identified those with close, dependent or ambivalent relationships as being 'at risk' as were those undergoing a concurrent stress at the time of bereavement. Research has also shown that a perceived low level of support is a risk factor in bereavement. These risk factors are now considered in more detail. They have implications for support of relatives during the person's terminal illness and their own bereavement.

Dependent or ambivalent relationships

In my hospice research, several future widowers had close, mutually dependent relationships with their wives in the sense that they were always together and seemed to have few close relationships outside marriage. In other instances, long-standing marital problems may present difficulties to the surviving person during bereavement. Where difficulties in relationships are long-standing, positions have often become entrenched and difficult to change. Help may best be given by not taking sides and by pointing to the positive features in the relationship, past or present, whenever possible. We may be able to encourage family members to act differently in small ways and this may help the relationship overall. For example, we could encourage a husband to show affection to his wife more openly, by telling her, perhaps for the first time, that he appreciates all she has done for him. If we have endeavoured to listen to the patient and various individual relatives, there will be less temptation to label particular people as 'difficult'. Where there are disputes in the family about who should visit and when, the patient's wishes should be noted and respected.

Concurrent stresses

Sometimes relatives have to cope with more than one sick person in the family, or a recent bereavement as well as the impending death of the patient. Such people will need particular understanding if they are to cope with the compounded stress such situations produce.

'I can't remember all of it, because I think my brain was put into neutral. Certainly the sister, I think, had gone through the experience. She was saying "You'll have the up days and the down days and it'll suddenly hit you sometimes if you see a photograph or if you're going through clothes or something. It'll spark off a memory." I find it difficult to visualise my father in his last days. I can only remember the good days. So her experience was true for myself.'

It is important to remember that people who have ambivalent relationships often have difficulties in bereavement. The son in the case quoted above, had few distressing or negative memories of his father. However, nurses may need to help people express their negative feelings of anger, guilt and resentment, as well as those of sorrow, loss and gratitude, by their own accepting and non-judgemental approach. Talking to relatives about the experience of bereavement and how they may feel at this time may help them to cope with the low points later on in their bereavement.

ADJUSTING TO AN ENVIRONMENT IN WHICH THE DYING PERSON IS MISSING

Many people have begun to cope alone while their relative is still alive because they recognise the need to take on new roles and responsibilities. This is true not only for relatives of cancer patients but for families of people with longer-term illnesses such as strokes and motor neurone disease. We should talk to relatives about these changes and how they feel they are going to cope, and honestly explore their capacity to cope. If relatives are helped to explore their plans for the future, even if only tentatively, their options may become clearer to them and possible consequences come to light which had not been considered previously. It may sometimes be easier for relatives to discuss future plans with an outsider, rather than a family member who might pressurise them into making particular decisions which might not be their wish.

Low perceived support

Perceived support is often more important than actual support in determining the outcome of a bereavement. People who perceive themselves as being unsupported, may be unable to accept support when it is offered. In my hospice research, most relatives seemed well supported, but a few perceived themselves as not having much support. These were mainly people who had had long and close marriages. Single people and close friends may be overlooked when assessing support. For example, an unmarried daughter may have been living with an elderly parent for many years and may have lost many of her own social contacts with her parent's increasing dependence. Unmarried sisters and brothers may have spent a lifetime together. For these people, the dying person may be as much at the centre of their existence as a husband or wife. There may be a long period after the person's death when they will feel intense loneliness. They may be helped, however, by the gentle and unobtrusive support of friends and relatives.

If we are aware of such friends and relatives, we may be able to suggest to them ways in which they could make their support more effective. We can stress the helpfulness of a sympathetic, listening ear and of acceptance of the importance of their loss. Practical help with shopping and preparation of meals may be important for elderly people. The bereaved person may have become socially isolated and need to develop social contacts with both sexes.

Other avenues of support should be explored with a view to the future, since the relative may not feel able to accept them immediately after the person's death, e.g. church connections, lunch clubs, home help services. Spiritual help may give great comfort to some relatives. A word with the chaplain or clergyman about funeral arrangements is usually helpful. Relatives who have no church connections may fear an impersonal funeral where the minister or priest knows neither the patient nor the family.

BEREAVEMENT FOLLOW UP

At St Columba's Hospice, a weekly team meeting is held to try to identify relatives who might be having a difficult bereavement and who need extra support. Such an assessment is subjective and is made by doctors and nurses (and sometimes other team members) who knew the bereaved relative either at home or at the hospice. General practitioners are notified if the team feels concerned about a particular relative. The relative could, if he or she wished, be put in touch with CRUSE, a national organisation for the bereaved. There are now a number of other support groups for the bereaved, e.g. The Stillbirth and Neonatal Death Society (SANDS) and The Compassionate Friends. The latter organisation is for parents who have lost a child. Society, as well as individuals, is developing expertise in supporting the bereaved in other traumatic situations, e.g. after the Bradford football stadium fire.

It is possible, even during a short interview with relatives to elicit important factors which may affect bereavement outcome. We should be aware that time spent talking to relatives and exploring these areas is likely to lead to a more accurate assessment of relatives' needs for support from us during the terminal illness and from professional colleagues and voluntary organisations during bereavement.

In this chapter I have tried to show how much can be done to prepare relatives for bereavement during the person's terminal illness as well as at the time of death. Just as the dying person may experience different emotional phases in coming to terms with his illness, so his relatives and close friends begin a grieving process which will continue into bereavement. There are many opportunities to help relatives in these 'tasks of mourning'. If we are also aware of those relatives who may be 'at risk' during bereavement, we can offer them extra support ourselves, put them in touch with professional colleagues or with a voluntary organisation such as CRUSE which specialises in meeting their needs.

Questions and exercises

1. How do you help relatives to prepare for bereavement? Do you help them in any of the ways mentioned in this chapter? i.e.

    (a) Helping them towards acceptance of the terminal diagnosis and prognosis.

    (b) Encouraging them to recognise and express their emotions.

    (c) Suggesting practical ways of helping them to adjust to changes in life style, role, etc.

    Add your own suggestions, based on your own experience.

2. How do you support relatives at the time of a patient's death? Do you discuss any of the following matters with them?

    (a) What has been written on the death certificate.

    (b) Registering the death and funeral arrangements.

    (c) Their own feelings at the time of death.

    (d) How they may feel during bereavement.

    (e) A commitment to counselling support if they wish it.

3. Do you use any informational leaflets in supporting bereaved relatives? In what ways might such leaflets be useful? Suggest some improvements to the material you have used in the past.

4. How do you identify relatives in need of extra support from you and your colleagues both during the terminal illness and during their bereavement?

5. What arrangements, if any, do you make for follow up of the bereaved, either by yourself or others?

Making communication   7
more effective

In our personal lives we are aware that our most meaningful communications take place in the context of warm and trusting relationships. As nurses, we should try, therefore, to relate to dying people and their relatives on a personal as well as a professional level. Thompson, Melia and Boyd (1983) described the relationships which can develop between dying people and professional carers as 'covenant' relationships, in contrast to the code and contract relationships more appropriate in other situations.* Carers are at the limit of what they can do in a curative sense and they offer the patient palliative care, support and befriending. By encouraging dying people to be involved in decisions about their own care and treatment whenever possible, they ensure that those aspects of care which enhance quality of life receive priority.

Nursing theory now stresses the importance of a person rather than a task-orientated approach to patients and their relatives. An essential part of individualised care for the dying is good communication between patient, relatives and staff. Stedeford (1981) found that patients in a continuing care unit were satisfied with the communication nursing staff had had with themselves and with their relatives because staff took time to listen to them.

'In the unit, patients were impressed by the fact that staff have time to talk and listen and usually did so on a one-to-one basis. They appreciated the willingness of staff to meet other family members and on occasion take the initiative in approaching them.'

* When a relationship is governed by contract, the person in need can make his own decisions, and can seek help elsewhere. Both the carer and the person in need have contractual rights and duties towards one another.
  When a relationship is governed by code, the carers have to decide what is in the best interests of the person in their care because the person is unable to make decisions for himself.

A similar description emerges from a study by C. and J. Parkes (1984) in which they compare terminal cancer care in 1967–69 with care in 1977–79 as evaluated by surviving spouses of patients who died in St Christopher's Hospice and other local hospitals.

'As in 1969, ward sisters and nurses in both settings were seen as "approachable", "friendly", "helpful" and "efficient", but there was a significant drop in the proportion of ward sisters who were seen as "very busy" from 60 per cent to 15 per cent at St Christopher's Hospice and from 92 per cent to 64 per cent elsewhere.'

NON-VERBAL COMMUNICATION

The importance of non-verbal communication in conveying to patients and relatives an impression of 'busyness' or 'availability', is

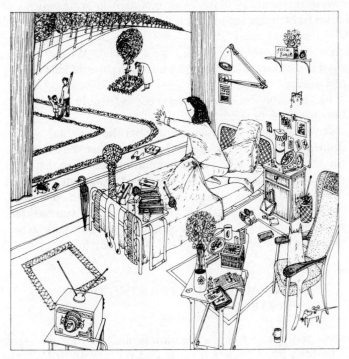

shown in the example above. It is important to make patients and relatives feel at home and to minimise the institutional character of the establishment. C. and J. Parkes' (1984) respondents characterised St Christopher's Hospice as being 'like a family'. My own research showed that a personal approach by nurses to patients and relatives is appreciated.

'I like how you feel at ease. Everybody is friendly.'

First impressions are important.

'My wife was naturally apprehensive but she came and immediately had a sense of well-being. I had maybe a five minute wait in reception and a comforting cup of tea that's obviously always given. Then I went into the ward and spoke to my wife and she was equally well comforted. When I looked at her bed and saw the flowers and the card with her name written on it and knowing that the emergency call had only gone to her doctor an hour before, I thought it was wonderful.'

INFORMALITY: BREAKING DOWN BARRIERS

Patients and relatives appreciate an informal, friendly atmosphere and facilities which enable them to feel relaxed. In St Columba's

Hospice there is a room where light refreshments are available and this is important for relatives who are visiting for most of the day. There is also a rest room where relatives can stay overnight, talk to the doctor in privacy, or simply be together as a family. Such simple, practical facilities are becoming more available in general hospitals and can do much to promote a feeling of welcome to relatives who are tired and under stress but who wish to remain close to their loved ones. A relative comments.

'It's a relaxed atmosphere. It's easy to visit. It's small and
people have got time.'

Use of first names

In my research, several relatives commented on the way that nurses called patients by their first names and how this helped them to relax. People are, of course, asked about their wishes in this matter when they are admitted and their preferences are respected. There is often reciprocal use of first names between nurses and patients so putting the relationship on an equal basis and avoiding 'parent-child' overtones. This can be an integral part of the personal approach by nurses to patients and relatives, as the following examples show.

Example 1
'The staff are all so friendly. It's important to talk and feel
that you're friends rather than nurse and patient. It's like a
family and for my wife and myself who have got no children,
it's really a family.'

Example 2
'They had "Bob" on a little sign above his bed. It's a tiny
thing, but again it gives you some feeling of warmth in the
place rather than just the surname. Little things like that
helped.'

Example 3
'The first names helped a lot. For the nurses my father was
"David" from the first moment he came in and several of the
nurses knew my mother's name, Peggy. She liked that. She
felt it was friendly.'

Like their relatives, many patients are apprehensive about admission to the Hospice since it indicates that they are entering the final stages of their illness. Once they have overcome their initial anxieties about admission, however, most patients seem to be able to relax a little and their most common comment is satisfaction with the individual care and attention they receive. Patients often say that they feel safe in the Hospice and their reassurance seems to derive from the perceived availability of staff and their ability to relieve distressing symptoms.

AVAILABILITY, CONSISTENCY AND COUNSELLING SKILLS

In a study of the Macmillan Nursing Service in West Lothian, Rutherford and McCleod (1986) stress the importance of availability, consistency and personal counselling skills in the relationships of Macmillan Nurses to the patient and relatives at home. Relatives had found such support more helpful than practical advice, although the latter was also appreciated.

Availability

In a hospice too the availability of the home care sisters is appreciated. It encourages a feeling in relatives and patients that expert help is always at hand, the sister being someone whom they know well, who is aware of their situation and who can be called upon when needed. Availability seems to be more important than frequent visiting, although the latter is appreciated. One relative felt able to cope as long as there was someone to turn to when things became too difficult at home.

'I had Dr Douglas and Sister Mary. They listened to me.
They gave me the feeling, "When you can't manage, let us
know and we'll be there." I'd always the feeling that
someone's there and you can say "Look, I've come to the
end now".'

The emotional rather than the physical strain of caring for the dying person at home is sometimes commented upon by relatives.

'The home care service helped mentally and in contact with
the family. It was reassuring for my sister and I to know that

someone was there to call on if things got too much. I think
mentally, rather than physically, was the way the home care
nurses helped. We felt somebody was taking an interest in
us. They went out of their way to phone you and let you
know what was happening. It made you feel safer.'

Relatives feel they can contact the home care team whenever they
are in difficulties without their anxieties appearing trivial. This gives
them extra confidence in caring for the dying person at home and
often extends the duration of such home care.

'You're all alone and you can't really phone up the GP. You
don't want to get embarrassed by asking silly questions. It
was nice when Mary, the home care sister, came down
because we could speak to her. She was like part of the
family, just coming in and knowing everybody that was
there. She was easy to speak to. I had a better idea of what
was going on. I thought that was good and I think it helped
Mum too.'

The quality of the relationship that patients and relatives have with
the home care sisters is ofen commented upon. They are described as
being 'relaxed', 'easy to speak to', 'supportive' and 'friendly'.

In St Columba's Hospice too, relatives mention the availability of
nursing staff to talk to them as being very important. Relatives feel
that the nurses try to get to know them when they come to visit.

Example 1

'They seem to know you here, although it's only the third
time I've been. First of all, there's more nurses here, but it's
the same ones you see when you come in.'

It is important for nurses and doctors to take the initiative in
communicating with patients and relatives.

Example 2

'I've spoken to the sisters two or three times. I've spoken to
one of the doctors and one or two of the nurses. The nurses
sometimes come across and sit beside us when we're with
father.'

Example 3

'Before I used to be frightened to talk to anyone like a

doctor. I feel that here you can relax and I'm not a relaxing person. The whole staff is so relaxed. I spoke to Dr Brown yesterday and he wasn't in a hurry to get away.'

Relatives are helped if they feel that nurses know them as a family and are aware of their circumstances, as the following examples show. One woman who had recently been bereaved describes the attitude of the nurses towards her parents.

Example 4

'The staff were so kind. Mother was quite touched that the nurse who was with father at the end was quite upset with her. I think people were prepared to talk. The male nurse spoke to her for quite a while one night.'

A young man was concerned because his mother was asking to go home, a situation he could not cope with because he and his wife had had a baby daughter ten days previously. He particularly appreciated the doctor taking the initiative in approaching him to discuss the problem.

Example 5

'One of the doctors came over and asked if she could see me for ten minutes. She said it wasn't the Hospice that had suggested that Mum went home. She said they would only send her home if she was well enough to go. When she was in the hospital, the hospital was quite free with the information, but you had to ask the right questions and you got the answers. I certainly appreciated being put in the picture and she did say if I had any concern to call into her office in passing or phone in.'

Telephone communications

The ready availability of information and support by telephone can greatly alleviate relatives' anxieties. We should encourage relatives to telephone as often as they wish for an updating on a patient's condition, or to get details of his daily activities and general well-being as this increases their sense of security. In a busy general hospital, it is helpful to staff if one relative maintains the telephone contact and relays the information to other family members. However, this may not be possible when a patient has a large family and many friends or when communication within the family is poor. We should ask relatives, on admission, whom we should contact if there is any deterioration in the patient's condition. If the next of kin is an elderly person or in poor health, for example, a son or daughter may wish to be telephoned first in order to break the news more gently to a parent. It is useful to keep a daily record of each patient's activities and any fluctuations in mood, as part of the documentation for the nursing care plan. Relatives appreciate information about whether the patient is eating his meals, sleeping well, or getting up in the mornings. Relatives often mention the helpfulness of telephone communication.

Example 1
'I usually phone before I go to bed at night and I phone in the morning. It's very comforting to feel he's all right.'

Example 2
'I phoned last night and this morning and this afternoon. Everyone has been very helpful.'

Consistency

One or two nurses should try to develop a deeper relationship with each patient and his or her relatives so that they are given an opportunity to discuss any anxieties with someone known and trusted. If relationships are built up more gradually in this way, patients and relatives feel more able to confide more fully their feelings and anxieties. If too many nurses are involved in the care, patients and relatives may only be able to relate to them in a fairly superficial way. In the community, both patients and relatives like having the same nurse to visit, as they feel that she is interested in how they are coping with the situation, as well as monitoring the patient's progress. Consistency is more difficult to achieve in a hospital or hospice setting where a number of nurses and other professionals are involved in care over a 24 hour period.

Counselling skills

The support of patients and relatives requires both sensitivity and counselling skills if it is to be effective. An essential element of counselling is that people are helped to adopt personal methods of coping with new experiences. For example, although many people experience the emotional reactions to loss described by Elizabeth Kubler Ross (1970), patients and relatives will respond with their own styles of coping, in the light of their own personality, previous experiences with illness and loss, and their experiences of relationships with family and with health professionals. As nurses we need to be skilled at helping patients and relatives to explore their feelings and anxieties and to identify their main concerns from among the many debilitating fears associated with terminal illness. One man particularly feared the effects on his wife of secondaries from a lung cancer.

'The doctor told me how her trouble is working and so forth.
He said they would do their best to make it peaceful for her.
He told us how the tumour will affect her and how he thinks
it should go, and he told us about the stages towards the
end. I felt better after he had talked to me.'

The ventilation of emotions is an important need of dying people and their relatives. There is a corresponding need for support from both nurses and other family members. Patients and relatives need opportunities to express their feelings and talk about family problems and other difficulties they are experiencing (see Chapter 5). In our relationships with patients and relatives we should help people to identify their strengths and the family, professional, and other resources available to them in coping with their situation. For example, dying people and their relatives may need help in coping with extreme anxiety and fear of the future. Some relatives have a great fear of being unable to cope with the patient's terminal illness and with their own future during bereavement.

As nurses we should consider our willingness to respond in a personal as well as professional way to the challenges and difficulties presented by families when a loved one is dying.

I have described the relationships with nurses that dying people and their relatives seem to find most supportive. The most valued features are availability, consistency and a counselling approach to support. Availability entails more than physical presence. It means having a familiar person to turn to in any kind of difficulty, great or small. Telephone support can greatly increase the availabiility of professional help. If one or two nurses take responsibility for supporting each dying person and his relatives, this allows for continuity and consistency of dialogue and for a deeper relationship to develop in which there is opportunity to confide in someone known and trusted. Such a 'covenant' relationship between the dying person and his carers goes beyond the normal contractual relationship between counsellor and client or professional and patient, since it entails a willingness to listen and befriend without imposing duties on the patient. However, counselling skills are vital so that people can be helped to adopt personal methods of coping with their situations and so that nurses can respond to each person's needs on an individual basis.

Questions and exercises

1. In what ways do you make yourself more approachable/available to communicate with dying people and their relatives (a) in the community or (b) in hospital? What do you do well? How could you improve the situation?
2. How could you minimise the 'institutional' character of a hospital ward and enable dying people and their relatives to feel more 'at home'?
3. In what ways could you improve 'consistency' or 'continuity' in relationships with dying people and their families?
4. To what extent would you describe your relationship with dying people as a 'covenant' relationship? Is that an honest assessment?

Potential communication 8
problems

Getting close to terminally ill people can be emotionally draining for their carers, although, in my own experience, forming supportive relationships with distressed relatives can be even more demanding. The temptation is to protect ourselves from 'overinvolvement' by distancing behaviour such as talking to colleagues instead of to patients or unconsciously controlling communication with patients and relatives so that people have little opportunity to express their real fears or negative feelings, such as anger or depression.

In terminal care, it is particularly important that stress experienced by patients and relatives should not be increased by poor communications, yet research has revealed, and our own personal and professional experience confirms, that great improvements are needed before patients and relatives receive the support which they have a right to expect from us.

POOR COMMUNICATION IN TERMINAL CARE

Regrettably, several studies have confirmed that many nurses' experiences of poor communication and support are widespread. For example, the Nuffield Provincial Hospitals Trust (1978) noted increasing concern with the practical consequences of failures in communication between patients, relatives and professionals in the National Health Service. Thompson (1979) writing about a report by CRUSE to a multidisciplinary working party, noted a lack of understanding of the need for privacy in hospital when someone was dying and that this was a concern to bereaved relatives. Nurses were criticised for the delivery of death messages to relatives, especially by phone. The bereaved had complained of phone calls saying that a person had died, without establishing whether the recipient of the information was alone or was able to get to the hospital. In my own

74

research, some relatives expressed considerable anger at what they perceived to be inadequate communication from doctors or nurses.

Example 1
'I've been kept in the dark. I made a fool of myself saying "There's no cancer" and there is. I'm really disillusioned. I'm very, very hurt.'

Example 2
'My father was in several hospitals and we met a lot of people. I had little faith in the ones I spoke to. I'd speak to different people and get different responses. They were over-worked and understaffed. I wanted somebody to sit down and talk to me and I wanted one person that I felt I could trust.'

Some of the reasons for this apparent difficulty in supporting the terminally ill and their relatives will now be considered.

Nurses' attitudes to terminal care

An awareness of our own attitudes to death and bereavement, acceptance of our vulnerability and need for personal support will help us to approach dying patients and their relatives in a spirit of willingness to listen, to offer support when we can, and to admit that we do not have all the answers to their problems. Thompson (1979) considered that communications between nurses and dying people would be greatly improved if nurses were better educated about death and dying, were better informed about the patient and their family circumstances, and if emotional support were provided for them from professional colleagues.

'If nurses are aware of their own and the patient's reactions to death, then they should be able to more realistically approach the task of using communication in assisting the patient to cope with his approaching death. Listening to the patient is far more important than talking to him and by listening, nurses will gain an understanding of his needs and worries.'

A study by Hockley (1983) demonstrated the importance of nurses sharing their experiences of caring for the dying and receiving support from colleagues.

'The student nurses felt unable to cope with the psychosocial aspects of caring for terminally ill patients, emphasising especially the relatives. They would like more ward-based teaching as well as classroom teaching, earlier on in their training.'

Birch (1979) found that among the most stressful aspects of nursing for first and third year students were nursing patients in pain, nursing the dying and talking to relatives of dying people. Anxiety about caring for the terminally ill and their relatives is not, of course, confined to student nurses. Many experienced professionals, doctors, nurses and clergy, have painful memories of bereavements and these make it difficult to care for patients and relatives who remind them of these experiences.

Inadequate communication skills

The development of counselling as a recognised professional specialism has shown that, although communication skills can be innate and that some people are naturally good communicators, new skills can also be learned and old ones improved upon. The Nuffield Provincial Hospitals Trust Working Party (1978) reviewed extensive

research on communications within the NHS and found evidence of poor medical interviewing and a lack of communication skills. In particular, they criticised the use of strings of routine questions which inhibited communication and the use of leading or closed questions which did not encourage patients to talk about their experiences of illness. A large study of general practitioners' interviews by Byrne and Long (1976) showed that most of them used a doctor rather than a patient-centred style and that the doctor did most of the talking. The need for a patient-centred approach is obviously relevant to nursing as well as to medicine. The importance of allowing the patient or the relative to lead communication exchanges cannot be overemphasised. Only then will they be able to express their concerns when they wish to do so and ask for information and support when they perceive that they need it. The question then changes from 'What to tell?' and 'When to tell?' to 'What does the patient want to know?' and 'At what pace can he cope with the knowledge?'

Time: quality and quantity in communications

Adequacy of communications is not only influenced by the time or numbers of staff available, but also, as has been indicated, by nurses' attitudes and communication skills. Quality is more important than quantity. In Hockley's study (1983), time for nurses to get involved with patients and their families was often curtailed by lack of continuity of care due to the rapid changeover of medical and nursing staff. There is a need for nurses to make an assessment of patients' physical, psychological and social needs and the needs of their relatives for support. It is unlikely that all these needs will be met in a single interview at the time of admission or on the initial referral to the community nurse. A supportive relationship between nurse and relatives will not be developed when contacts are fleeting, hurried, or subject to interruption. My own experience has shown that a comparatively short time set aside to talk to patients and relatives and to listen to their concerns is greatly appreciated. There may be moments when a patient or relative feels particularly vulnerable and needs to express anxieties and fears. Experienced nurses will be aware that such moments often seem to occur when, for instance, the patient is having a bath or other intimate procedure carried out and when defences are lowered. These opportunities to share deep feelings should always be encouraged by nurses since, if they are ignored, they may not recur.

Interprofessional communication

Interprofessional communication can improve or hinder the psychological support which can be given to patients and relatives by the caring team. Sofaer (1983) showed the importance of mutual communication between doctors and nurses in achieving pain control in surgical wards. Community nurses will recognise the importance of good communication between themselves and the hospital when a patient is discharged home. Unfortunately, the accompanying note often details the diagnosis and treatment given but gives no indication of what the patient and relatives have been told about the illness or prognosis. Until the note from the hospital arrives explaining the position or a telephone call is made to the ward, the primary care team may be in the embarrassing position of trying to discover what the patient and family know. In this interval, damage can be done as the nurse will know the diagnosis and, possibly by non-verbal communication, gives the patient cause for concern. In giving ongoing emotional support to patient and family and responding to their day-to-day needs, good communication between doctors, nurses and other professionals is essential as is the recognition that each profession has an important contribution to make. Frequent team meetings should be held to discuss the needs of dying patients and their families. In Hockley's study (1983), it was noted:

'Some of the senior nurses in particular were very well
motivated to try to incorporate principles of hospice care into
the acute medical situations. . . . Often though, because of
pressure of work and inexperience of symptom control, they
lacked the necessary confidence when confronted with
medical personnel.'

It is too readily accepted by nurses that the prime responsibility for achieving good symptom control is medical. However, confrontational methods of communication between nurses and doctors are not helpful in resolving problems for the patient's benefit. For example, nurses should accept responsibility in reporting a patient's pain and in monitoring the effects of analgesics. The patient's assessment of pain control using a pain chart may be more objective, detailed and less opinionated than the nurse's 'view' on the patient's drug regime. A nurse prepared to listen to patients and report their questions and anxieties, helps to avoid an unnatural distinction between 'telling' and 'not telling' patients about their condition.

Communicating with 'difficult' patients and relatives

Nurses may find certain patients 'difficult' to relate to for a variety of reasons. Stockwell's study (1984) of the unpopular patient found that nurses spent less time communicating with such people because they were demanding of their time and unrewarding as they were unappreciative of what was done for them. Dying people may try to cope with their anxieties and fears by being demanding or clinging, by complaining or sometimes by developing obsessional habits like keeping a note of all the medicines they receive and of the progress of their symptoms.

Some patients and relatives may become very withdrawn and uncommunicative. One such patient at the hospice, a young man, was greatly helped by a nurse who sat on his bed and talked to him whenever she had the opportunity. Although he only replied in monosyllables at first, he gradually became more responsive.

Initiating communication

Some patients and relatives are reserved about approaching staff and speaking to them, especially when they are perceived as being very busy. It can be difficult, even in a relaxed atmosphere, for them to take the initiative in approaching staff. Patients and relatives may also be confused about nurses' uniforms and unsure of who best to approach. The following examples from my own research illustrate some of these difficulties from the relatives' viewpoint.

Example 1
'I've spoken to the nurses if they've been at the bedside or on the verandah. I've not really approached them to be quite honest. I leave it to them.'

Example 2
'I haven't spoken to anyone yet. I'm a bit shy.'

Example 3

'I haven't spoken to the doctor on his own yet. It's difficult
when my husband's there. He would want to know what we
were talking about.'

One relative requested that the nurses take more initiative in
communicating.

Example 4

'I think it's important that someone speaks to the relative
every other day or something like that.'

Relatives may sometimes be neglected, even when communication
with the patient is good. Relatives may not be present when the doctor
speaks to the patient, so a situation may easily arise where a person has
been in hospital or hospice for several days before the relative has
spoken to a member of staff. At St Columba's Hospice, there is a
system of 'starring' a patient's name when his condition has
deteriorated or when the nurse or doctor wants to speak to the
relatives. The receptionist then ensures that they do not leave before
seeing the doctor or nurse.

OBTAINING THE REQUIRED SUPPORT

People communicate their deeper anxieties and fears in the context of
a relationship of trust. It was this personal support which patients and
relatives found so helpful with the home care service. One relative
commented:

'At the moment, there's so many nurses I haven't figured
them all out. I found the home care were very helpful. If I
was really upset, I would go to Sister Sheila (home care). I've
had that connection with her.'

A few relatives commented that they would have liked a member of
the nursing staff to sit and talk to them and allow them an opportunity
for questions. These relatives felt that the nurses were friendly and
approachable but that they needed support at a deeper level. The
following examples reveal relatives' desire for more support and
information from nursing staff. Again their perceptions of the staff's
'busyness' seem to deter relatives from approaching nurses.

Example 1

'I've only chatted to the nurses, sort of informal pleasantries and so on.'

Example 2

'I recognise the nurses and speak to them in passing but they're a bit busy when I'm there; they seem busy.'

Example 3

'I just don't know anything. I know they can't put a time on it. I'm supposed to be going on holiday in a fortnight's time. I decided not to go. I just asked sister if the doctor had spoken to her and what he said. You don't want to be bothering them. They're busy and they've got a lot to do.'

Example 4

'I haven't had any discussions with the nursing staff. If I've any criticisms it's that. If someone after two days said, "Oh Mrs Y, can we see you for a few minutes", but nobody in fact has. Nobody actually stopped me and said "You know, we are doing X, Y, Z". That might have been helpful.'

COMMUNICATING SPIRITUAL NEEDS

The issue of how to help people who fear death rather than suffering or the process of dying is a difficult one. For some, it raises questions about the meaning of life and of their own lives in particular. Julia Neuberger (1987) explored these issues in the first volume in this series. There may be moments when staff feel that a person is seeking more than relief from suffering and that the questions asked are essentially spiritual, although they may not be expressed in such a way. Staff should not feel hesitant about trying to give spiritual help and sharing their own beliefs if they feel that the patient is asking and such a sharing would be appropriate. Those who feel unable to respond on a personal level can work with their colleagues or with the clergy for the benefit of the patient. It is important that staff do not have 'no go areas' so far as communication is concerned. In my own research, a few patients seemed to remain unhappy and anxious despite the efforts of staff to help them. Some of these were worried by the death of other patients as this seemed to be a reminder of their own mortality and one patient was also upset by the sight of other ill people. A patient's unhappiness obviously affects their relatives. Such spiritual pain is not alleviated if attention is paid only to people's physical needs, however good the standard of care.

I have outlined some familiar communication problems in terminal care. When such difficulties arise, solutions may depend on asking ourselves the right questions. For example, communication is a dialogue, hence the need to be aware of what patients and relatives want to know as well as being concerned with how and what we should tell them. Some difficulties in communication may be more apparent to the staff than perceived by patients and relatives. For example, a heavy workload may mean that less time can be spent with patients and relatives than we would wish. However, meaningful and effective communications need not necessarily be lengthy. Indeed, some of us who have been on the receiving end of long-winded monologues in which we found it difficult to state our own views, would readily recognise that brevity can be a virtue! So long as we give equal priority to communication as we do to other aspects of care and realise that support can be planned and evaluated we will not go far wrong. Interprofessional communication takes place against a background of mutual role expectations, but such expectations can be changed and become more realistic if the professionals involved are more prepared to be open with each other and show greater understanding of each other's responsibilities.

Questions and exercises

1. How do you try to communicate with a terminally ill person who seems anxious, withdrawn or depressed? Are you usually successful? If not, why not?

2. Think back to the last time you had difficulties communicating with a dying person. What did you see as the problem areas for (a) him/her and (b) for you? What did you do well? In retrospect, how could you have been more supportive?

3. What do you feel is your role, if any, in talking to dying people or their relatives about spiritual matters?

A three-stage model 9
of support

Friendliness and warmth from professional staff are clearly appreciated by patients and relatives, but sometimes a deeper level of support is indicated. People under stress value having a sympathetic listener. Many also seek someone who will help them to clarify what they should do to cope more effectively with the difficulties brought about by serious illness. To be effective, the support of terminally ill people and their relatives requires an individual approach from nursing staff combined with counselling skills.

Counselling differs from other forms of 'helping' relationships in assisting people to help themselves by becoming aware of available choices, making their own decisions, or coming to terms with a new experience. Gerard Egan (1981) developed a skills model of counselling which, like the nursing process, has three stages. In the exploration stage the person is helped to assess his own situation and needs. This may take some time. A picture of patients' and relatives' needs can be built up over a number of interactions with the nurse, and any problems or anxieties they want to explore can be identified. In the understanding stage, the person is helped to reach a new understanding of his situation and to clarify what he might do to cope effectively. The third stage is helping the person to implement decisions and plans and consider possible consequences. A care plan for patient and relatives is made out. The nurse, as counsellor, can use her skill and experience to be aware that the person is ready to move from one stage to another, thus ensuring that she goes at the person's pace and not her own. When giving support, it is important to remember how easy it is for professionals to make such vulnerable people dependent upon them, and thereby to increase their sense of helplessness. Nurses can create difficulties for themselves by asking questions such as, 'What should the patient be told about his illness?' instead of, 'What does the patient want to know about his illness?' Support of patient and family should always be preceded by careful assessment of their expressed needs. This allows an individual and flexible approach to be

83

adopted for each person. The Egan model of counselling and support and its application to terminal care will now be examined in more detail. An outline of the model is shown below.

The Egan model of counselling (1981)

Establishing a relationship

Level 1 – exploring
Level 2 – understanding
Level 3 – action (and evaluation)

Closing contact

Establishing a relationship with patient and family

The first contact between nurse, patient and relative(s) will have an important influence on later relationships. Time, availability and privacy are important in establishing good relationships. In hospital, it is preferable if one or two nurses can take responsibility for the support of a particular patient and family to ensure continuity of dialogue and to build up a trusting relationship. Information important to the care of patient and family can be shared with members of the professional team. The nurse responsible for the care of a particular patient and family should take the initiative in sustaining contact with them, so letting them know that she has set time aside for any concerns they may want to discuss.

Timing of support sessions

Timing is important in establishing any relationship. Relatives and patients are often under stress at the time of admission to hospital, or on an initial home visit. They may be anxious about the suspected diagnosis or about signs of recurrence of an earlier disease. The hospital environment can be stressful in itself, presenting new and sometimes unpleasant experiences and a bewildering number of new faces to be remembered. Patients and relatives are often further confused by the variety of uniforms seen in hospital. Any session at this initial stage should be as brief as possible to minimise stress. A further session (or sessions) is, nevertheless, needed to explore patients' and relatives' needs and to plan emotional support. As the aim of the sessions is to allow dying people and their relatives to explore areas of concern to them, it should be made clear from the outset that there is no set agenda for discussion nor any information which must be obtained. If family communications seem to be blocked in any way, it may be helpful to talk to patient and family together.

Hospital – community liaison

There may be considerable information available about the social circumstances of patients referred from community to hospital or vice versa. Some of this information may be invaluable in planning the giving of effective support, and good hospital–community liaison is important. For example, a note should be made of patients' and relatives' awareness of diagnosis, if appropriate. A family tree may be useful in identifying those relatives and friends of the patient who may need support. A visit by the community nurse to the hospital could provide hospital nurses with information about a patient's home circumstances, or help to prepare for discharge.

STAGE ONE

The first stage in developing supportive relationships would be an exploration of patients' and relatives' needs and anxieties conducted in an atmosphere where privacy and freedom from interruption are guaranteed. The skills demanded of the interviewer at this stage are as follows.
1. Active listening
2. Clarifying the main concerns
3. Responding to feelings

Active listening

By giving total attention to what the other person is saying about his experiences and feelings, the helper can create a climate of empathy and trust. The patient or relative should be encouraged to talk freely. They may want to talk about a problem that is worrying them or just express their feelings to a sympathetic listener. It is important to give people the chance to do this rather than to subject them to many questions initially. When not pressurised to respond to the nurse's agenda they will be more likely to present a fuller version of their various problems.

Clarifying the main concerns

Patients and relatives may respond to an invitation to talk by describing many anxieties or problems. It is important to find out which of these are the main concerns. Open questions encourage the person to develop an open and 'giving' conversation and explore thoughts and feelings, rather than giving brief, defensive responses. Gradually, as the session progresses, the helper can begin assisting the person to focus on the most important areas of concern (for the person, not the helper). For example, if relatives are anxious about coping at home, they could be asked to give examples of situations where they feel anxious. As the main concerns emerge, these can be explored in more depth in stage two of the interview.

Responding to feelings

Both patients and relatives experience emotions associated with grief, i.e. denial, anxiety, anger and guilt. They want the opportunity to express their feelings and to talk about the difficulties they are experiencing. Strong negative feelings which are not expressed can make coping with terminal illness significantly more difficult for patients and relatives. The nurse can help the person explore these often painful emotions by sensitive listening and reflecting of feelings. The person gets the chance to 'ventilate' feelings which, in itself, can bring a sense of relief, and also the person becomes more aware of the reasons behind these feelings.

STAGE TWO

At this stage, the person is helped to become as clear as possible about his concerns and what he might do to cope more effectively with them. The skills demanded of the helper are as follows.

1. Responding and leading
2. Promoting understanding
3. Information giving
4. Giving advice

Responding and leading

The helper directs the person's attention to areas that seem important to the person being interviewed.

Promoting understanding

The helper encourages the person to gain insight into his feelings and circumstances. As the dialogue progresses and mutual confidence and trust grow it is easier to ask more sensitive questions. For example, relatives of a dying person might be asked 'Have you thought at all about the future?' Many relatives are willing to talk about this and some will speak of tentative plans they are making. New understanding may help people to see patterns in their behaviour of which they were previously unaware. For example, a female relative who has been curt and irritable with nursing staff may begin to realise that she is angry with them for 'taking over' the care of her loved one, and making her feel inadequate and guilty. With new understanding, she begins to realise that she has often responded to serious events in her life by taking control, and that this has often antagonised people.

Information giving

Patients and relatives need information from staff at different stages of the illness and at a level with which they can cope. Information should only be given after assessing the patients' and relatives' desire for it. For example, some relatives do not want to know the patient's prognosis and many do not want detailed information about the terminal illness itself, symptoms or treatment. Relatives do, however, need frequent updating on the person's condition to allay their anxiety.

Giving advice

Advice should be given with caution, only when requested and when the patient's and relatives' situation has been explored. Relatives may ask for advice because they want a professional assessment of the situation and feel incompetent to make it themselves. There are dangers in giving specific advice when, for example, the patient's condition is uncertain. People who appear extremely ill may sometimes improve and live for several weeks or months. Other people may deteriorate suddenly and die just at the moment when the relative had decided to go home to rest.

STAGE THREE

Stage three of the interview involves identifying possible actions and their respective implications for support by professionals. Fairly immediate action is sometimes indicated and the help of the nursing staff may be required. For example, there may be problems of communication in some families or parents may be concerned about what to tell the children about the terminal illness. The skills required of the helper at this stage are as follows.
1. Planning action
2. Anticipating situations

Planning action

Patients and relatives are encouraged to consider what they might do to alleviate any problems, to attain important goals and improve their quality of life. Staff may be able to help in this. For example, a patient may wish to make out a will to ensure adequate provision for his family, or relatives may wish to plan a special celebration for the patient's birthday or for a wedding anniversary.

Anticipating situations

In some areas, patients or relatives may not be in a position to make definite decisions or plans. Some relatives have to experience bereavement before they know how they will cope with, for example, role changes or moving house. Nevertheless, they will be in a better position to make wise decisions, having had the opportunity to discuss their situation, consider alternatives and clarify their feelings beforehand.

ASSESSING THE LEVEL OF SUPPORT NEEDED

The support offered by empathy and a listening ear may be sufficient for some patients and relatives who may then feel more able to cope with their difficulties. However, the problems presented on first acquaintance with patients and relatives may recede in importance and others may assume greater significance. Assessment and support must, therefore, be ongoing to be effective. Maslow (1962) has described an ascending order of human needs from basic physical and security needs to needs for giving and receiving love and for self-development. These needs are just as much present in dying people as in those who have a long span of life ahead. A small study by Nimmo (1982) at St Columba's Hospice has reinforced an impression that though patients may present largely physical problems on admission, emotional, social and spiritual concerns emerge as important at later interviews. It may be that professional staff make priorities out of problems which they can solve therapeutically. In nursing, there has been an emphasis on the active work of giving physical care rather than on the equally demanding work of communicating with and giving support to patients and their families. Patients and their relatives and professional carers may perceive different priorities of care, hence the need for continuing support, so that all the concerns of patients and relatives are allowed to emerge.

CLOSING CONTACT

The supportive relationship between a nurse and a terminally ill person has a natural end when the person dies. In the support of bereaved relatives, however, there is not always an obvious time to begin closing contact. There are certain points to be considered which may prompt closing contact.

1. The person may have needs which the helper cannot meet. For example, there may be signs of abnormal grieving, such as severe depression or inability to make a beginning to a life without the deceased person.

2. The person may need referral to another agency or professional in order to receive appropriate help. For example, the bereaved person may need medical or psychiatric help.

3. If the helper is no longer able to continue to support the person, perhaps because of professional commitments, referral to another agency for further support might be appropriate. For example, a health visitor or district nurse might refer a bereaved person to a group such as CRUSE where both individual counselling and group support are available. Such a referral would, of course, only be made with the bereaved person's consent.

4. Contact may be closed when the aims of the supportive relationship seem to have been met. Sometimes this may be done gradually, with visits from the helper becoming less frequent as the person seems progressively more able to cope alone.

It may be difficult to close contact with a person whom we, as nurses, have grown to like and who is grateful for the care received from us. However, it is important to allow the person to grow in independence, and it is necessary for our own emotional well-being that we do not see ourselves as the only ones capable of giving such support. We also have obligations to other patients and relatives who may have a more pressing need for our help. The ability to close a supportive relationship successfully at the appropriate time is, therefore, as important as its establishment. The memory of both first and last impressions will probably remain with relatives for the rest of their lives.

An example of how the counselling model could be applied to the support of dying people and their relatives was given earlier, when a relative was described as being angry with the nurses for 'taking over' the care of her loved one. She can be helped to explore and gain insight into her feelings. In the action stage of the counselling session, she may decide that she needs to express more often how anxious, worried and lost she feels over her loved one's imminent death. She identifies a close friend who she thinks she can trust to confide in, and she decides to tell her how she feels the next time they meet. The counselling nurse explains how she can become more involved in the nursing of her husband, if she wishes, and that she can telephone the hospital whenever she feels anxious or wishes to be updated on his condition.

Areas to be explored with dying people and their relatives

The preceding chapters have indicated the areas of likely concern to dying people and their relatives and which should be explored with them by the nursing staff. These are now identified as follows.

Awareness of diagnosis: patients and relatives
Patients' and relatives' awareness of the terminal diagnosis should be noted. Any communication between patients, relatives and staff about the diagnosis or prognosis should be recorded so that continuity of emotional support can be given by the various professionals involved in the patient's care.

Coping with terminal illness: patients and relatives
Nurses should note how patients and relatives are coping with the terminal illness, since awareness does not always indicate acceptance. The principal carer should be identified, as the burden of care, both physical and emotional, may have taken its toll. Negative feelings in both patient and relative should be explored so that they can be helped to cope with their situation in as positive a manner as possible.

Anxiety
Areas of anxiety should be explored with both patients and relatives so that opportunities to alleviate these fears are not lost.

Perceived support: patients and relatives
The extent of perceived support seems to be more important than the size of a person's social network in alleviating loneliness. Opening up communications within the family of a terminally ill person can

increase the support members give to each other. Patients can often give great support to each other. For example, groups of patients who meet weekly at St Columba's day hospice, grow in understanding and their ability to support each other. Relatives who do not perceive themselves as being well supported seem to be more at risk of having a difficult bereavement. All these situations have implications for support from professional staff.

Planning action: the patient's priorities and plans

Stage three of the counselling process involves making plans which have been mutually agreed between patient and professional carer. Seemingly unimportant things can make an enormous difference to the quality of life of terminally ill people. If the nurse is aware of a patient's priorities, she can help him use his limited energies to maximum effect in the short time that may be left to him and create some happy memories for relatives. In cases where a very ill person has become withdrawn and uncommunicative with his family, relatives may need particular help and support so that they realise that this is not a rejection of them, but part of the illness.

Relatives' priorities and plans

When death has been anticipated for weeks or months, relatives have often begun to think of the future without the patient and some begin to make tentative plans. Where the terminal illness is at all protracted, relatives may have been obliged to adopt new roles and a new life style. For example, they may be considering moving house. Loss of income may mean changes in life style. When encouraging the relatives to think about and discuss their own needs, the nurse could discourage them from making overly hasty decisions based on their present feelings, and which they may later regret.

The aim in this chapter has been to indicate the needs of dying people and their relatives for an appropriate level of support from nursing staff. Some difficulties which terminally ill people and their relatives experience have been discussed and the implications for psychological support considered. It is not intended that only the nurse should be seen as giving this help. The support of colleagues in the professional team is essential. In Chapter 2, the importance of team meetings and case conferences in promoting mutual respect, cooperation and understanding among the various professionals was emphasised. Mutual respect and cooperation are necessary for any one team member to develop skills in counselling and support. The comments of colleagues from their own and other disciplines (and indeed from patients and relatives) can be invaluable in improving nurses' communication skills. A hierarchical approach to communication in terminal care with each member of a team taking his or her cue from the top of the professional hierarchy is unlikely to be helpful to patients and is stressful for staff concerned.

Nurses could make a more effective contribution to the provision of support to dying patients and their relatives, and the multi-disciplinary team should be constantly seeking to improve the level of its collective skills. If a team approach to the support of dying people and their relatives is accepted as necessary, there are obvious implications for nursing education, since nurses have a key role. The improvement of communication and counselling skills is now considered important for both student and registered nurses. More interdisciplinary counselling courses are needed to promote mutual awareness and understanding of roles among professionals.

A good team approach to care does not just happen. Its members have to work together and grow in mutual understanding, con-

fidence and support. Usually a doctor is the team leader but other members have important roles. A nurse may find that her role is that of coordinating the contributions of the various team members, for the benefit of the patient and family. For example, a district nurse will liaise with the GP, the Macmillan nurse, or the health visitor, and various agencies such as the home help service or the night sitter service, in providing care for the terminally ill person. Her active role as advocate of the patient is vital. Since she is often in daily contact with patient and family she is also best placed to be aware of their expressed needs. Very often a nurse, both in hospital and community, is the key person in communicating between the terminally ill person and family and professional carers. Nurses should be encouraged to expand their already growing contribution to this essential area of patients' and relatives' care, whether in the community, in hospital or in a hospice.

Questions and exercises

1. How do you plan emotional support for dying people and their relatives? What do you do well? Which areas of your support could be improved?
2. Which aspects of the Egan model of counselling might you find particularly helpful in improving your own communication in terminal care?
3. When talking to dying patients and their relatives, how much time do you spend
   (a) Listening – responding
   (b) Talking – leading
   What does this say about you?
4. When talking to dying people and their relatives how much time do you spend
   (a) Giving them advice
   (b) Giving them information
   (c) Asking them about their feelings, anxieties, problems.
   What does this say about you?
5. How do you help terminally ill people and relatives identify their priorities and make their own plans? What do you do well? How could you be more helpful to patients and relatives in this area?

6. Do you have any difficulties closing contact with bereaved relatives? In what ways could you make this easier?

Postscript

This book has been written openly about the caring of the terminally ill patient in hospices, in hospitals and at home. It covers many aspects of the worries, fears and anxieties of patients and relatives. It discusses the relationship between staff and patients in St Columba's Hospice and touches on subjects such as day visits, which familiarise the patient with the Hospice. It speaks of the relative's role when a loved one is being cared for in the Hospice and the need to be able to converse with staff at the Hospice. Simply to talk or ask questions which may be worrying the relative can lend support when a doctor or nurse with confidence and experience can speak frankly about the patient's condition. It also deals with family support in the bereavement itself. At the Hospice the 'caring' for the patient and the 'dignity' of the patient are factors which are highly important.

The Home Care Service and the Macmillan Nurses who play an important part in the Hospice caring service are also discussed in their role of visiting patients in their homes, dealing with their needs, and becoming familiar with relatives and the home circumstances.

From my own personal experience this care was given to my own family during my mother's illness and tremendous support was received. Each visit from the nurse was on a friendly basis when my mother and my family always felt at ease in discussing any problems. Questions were always frankly and honestly answered. There was always a feeling of 'trust' and a knowledge that my mother was in the hands of extremely qualified and sympathetic people.

Daughter of a patient

References

Birch, J. (1979) The anxious learners. *Nursing Mirror* **148**, Feb 8.

Byrne, P.S. and Long, E.L. (1976) *Doctors talking to patients: a study of verbal behaviour of general practitioners consulting in their surgeries.* HMSO, London.

Carkuff, R.R. (1969) *Helping and Human Relations: a Primer for Lay and Professional Helpers.* Holt, Rinehart and Winston, New York.

Egan, G. (1981) *The Skilled Helper: a model for systematic helping and interpersonal relating.* Brooks/Cole N.E., Monterey CA.

Glaser, B.G. and Strauss, A.L. (1965) *Awareness of Dying.* Aldine Publishing Co., Chicago.

Hampe, S.O. (1975) Needs of the grieving spouse in a hospital setting. *Nursing Research* **24**, 2, 113–120.

Hinton, J. (1972) *Dying.* Penguin Books, Harmondsworth, Middlesex, England.

Hockley, J. (1983) *An investigation to identify symptoms of distress in the terminally ill patient in the general medical ward.* City and Hackney Health District, Nursing Research Paper 2.

Jobling, M. (1975) *Bereavement in Childhood – A Summary of Research Findings.* National Children's Bureau Information Service, Highlight No 15, London EC1V 7QE.

Kubler Ross, E. (1970) *On Death and Dying.* Tavistock Publications Ltd., London.

Lewis, C.S. (1961) *A Grief Observed.* Faber and Faber, London.

Maguire, G.P. (1975) The psychological and social consequences of breast cancer. *Nursing Mirror* **140**, 14, 53–5.

Maslow, A. (1962) *Towards a Psychology of Being.* Van Nostrand Reinhold Co. Inc., New York.

McIntosh, J. (1977) *Communication and Awareness in a Cancer Ward.* Croom Helm Ltd., London.

Neuberger, J. (1987) *Caring for People of Different Faiths.* Austen Cornish Publishers Ltd., London.

Nimmo, G. (1982) *A study of the principal distresses experienced by patients with terminal cancer and the importance attached to them by patient and physician.* St Columba's Hospice, Edinburgh (unpublished).

Nuffield Provincial Hospitals Trust (1978) *Talking with Patients: A Teaching Approach.* Nuffield Provincial Hospitals Trust, London NW1.

Parkes, C. and J. (1984) Hospital versus hospice, a revaluation after 10 years as seen by surviving spouses. *Post Graduate Medical Journal* **60**, 120–124.

Raphael, B. (1984) *The Anatomy of Bereavement.* A Handbook for the Caring Professions. Anchor Brendon Ltd., Essex.

Rutherford, M. and McCleod, C. (1986) *The West Lothian Macmillan Service: The First Three Years.* Unpublished report.

Sofaer, B. (1983) Pain relief – the importance of communication. *Nursing Times,* December 7.

Speck, P. (1978) *Loss and Grief in Medicine.* Baillière Tindall, London.

Stedeford, A. (1981) Couples facing death: psychosocial aspects. *British Medical Journal* **283**, 1033–1036.

Stedeford, A. (1981) Couples facing death: unsatisfactory communications. British Medical Journal **283**, 1098–1101.

Stockwell, F. (1984) *The Unpopular Patient.* Croom Helm Ltd., London and Sydney.

Strachan, J.G. (1981) Reactions to bereavement: a study of a group of adult mentally handicapped hospital residents. *Journal of the British Institute of Mental Handicap* **9**, 1, 20–21.

Thompson, I. (Ed) (1979) *Dilemmas of Dying: A Study in the Ethics of Terminal Care.* Edinburgh University Press, Edinburgh. Appendix 1.

Thompson, I.E., Melia, K.M. and Boyd, K.M. (1983) *Nursing Ethics.* Churchill Livingstone, Edinburgh.

Wilson, C.M. (1985) Stress in Hospital Nursing, *The Division of Clinical Psychology Newsletter,* no. 48, June, British Psychological Society.

Winnicot, D.W. (1968) *The Family and Individual Development.* Social Science paperbacks.

Woodhall, C. (1986) A family concern. *Nursing Times and Nursing Mirror* **82**, 31–33.

Worden, W. (1984) *Grief Counselling and Grief Therapy.* Tavistock Publications Ltd., London.

Wright, K. and Dyck, S. (1984) Expressed concerns of adult cancer patients' family members. *Cancer Nursing,* October, 371–374.

Bibliography

Benjamin, A. (1981) *The Helping Interview*. (3rd Edn.) Houghton Mifflin Co., Boston, USA.

Calnan, J. (1983) *Talking with Patients*. William Heinemann Medical Books, London.

Munroe, E.A., Manthei, R.J. and Small, J.J. (1983) *Counselling: A Skills Approach*. Methuen Publications (NZ) Ltd., printed in Great Britain by J.W. Arrowsmith Ltd.

Useful addresses

Alzheimer's Disease Society
3rd Floor, Bank Building
Fulham Broadway
London SW6 1EP
Telephone: 01-381 3177

Raises funds to support hospices.

British Association for Cancer United Patients (BACUP)
121–123 Charterhouse Street
London EC1M 6AA
Telephone: 01-608 1785/6

Provides information for cancer patients and others; produces leaflets on various aspects of cancer; gives telephone support.

Cancer Link
46A Pentonville Road
London N1 9HF
Telephone 01-833 2451

Will put enquirers in touch with local cancer support groups throughout the country.

CARE (Cancer After-care and Rehabilitation Society)
Lodge Cottage
Church Lane
Timsbury
Bath BA3 1LF
Telephone: 0761 70731

Offers support and advice to cancer patients and their families, including information about hospices and welfare rights.

Compassionate Friends
5 Lower Clifton Hill
Clifton
Bristol BS8 1BT
Telephone: 0272 292778

Offer support and help for people suffering the loss of a child; leaflets for parents, professionals, friends and relatives and a library.

Crossroads (Association of Crossroads Care Attendance Scheme)
94 Coton Road
Rugby
Warwickshire CV21 4LN
Telephone: 0788 73653

Have schemes in various parts of the UK that allow families to have a break from caring at home for handicapped people.

CRUSE: National Organisation for Widowed and their Children
Cruse House
126 Sheen Road
Richmond
Surrey TW9 1UR
Telephone: 01-940 4818/9047

Counselling service with more than 100 branches throughout UK; wide range of literature.

Foundation for the Study of Infant Death
(Cot Death Research and Support Associations)
5th Floor, 4 Grosvenor Place
London SW1 7HD
Telephone 01-235 1721

Advice and counselling for newly bereaved parents; sponsors research and produces useful leaflets.

Gay Switchboard
BM Switchboard
London WC1N 3XX
Telephone: 01-837 7324

Twenty-four hour information and help service for lesbians and gay men; will also refer those recently bereaved to their bereavement project.

Jewish Bereavement Counselling Service
14 Chalgrove Gardens
London NW3 3PN
Telephone: 01-349 0839

Will send trained volunteer counsellors to bereaved; operates in Greater London but can refer to other projects and individuals elsewhere.

Malcolm Sargent Cancer Fund for Children
26 Lamont Road
London SW10 0JE
Telephone: 01-352 6805

Can provide cash grants to parents of children with cancer to help pay for clothing, equipment, etc. (Hospital social worker can supply application form).

Marie Curie Memorial Foundation
28 Belgrave Square
London SW1X 8QG
Telephone: 01-235 3325

Advisory and counselling service for cancer patients and relatives; can provide day and night nursing service for patients at home and runs welfare grant scheme.

Motor Neurone Disease Association
32 Hazelwood Road
Northampton NN1 1LN
Telephone: 0604 22269

Gives advice and information for sufferers of this disease; grants for
home nursing, hospice care and holidays; leaflets available.

National Association for Widows (NAW)
c/o Stafford and District Voluntary Service Centre   .
Chell Road
Stafford ST16 2QA
Telephone: 0785 45465

Advice and support for widows; pressure group fighting against
financial anomalies that widows have to face.

National Society for Cancer Relief
Anchor House
15/19 Britten Street
London SW3 3TY
Telephone: 01-351 7811

Support, advice and help concerning terminal cancer; provides
short-stay homes and nursing services for patients; can provide
financial help for those in need; apply through social worker, GP or
social services.

St Christopher's Hospice Information Service
51–59 Lawrie Park Road
Sydenham
London SE26 6DZ
Telephone: 01-778 9252

Can provide information about approximately 87 hospices in the
UK.

Stillbirth and Neonatal Death Society (SANDS)
Argyle House,
29–31 Euston Road
London NW1 2SD
Telephone: 01-833 2851

Offers advice and long-term support, via local groups, to newly bereaved parents of stillbirths and/or of babies who die in their first month of life.

Sue Ryder Foundation
Cavendish
Sudbury
Suffolk CO10 8AY
Telephone: 0787 280252

Runs 20 homes for the physically handicapped and for both terminal and convalescent cancer patients; can also provide domiciliary care teams.

Tenovus Cancer Information Service
11 Whitchurch Road
Cardiff CF4 3JN
Telephone: 0222 619846

Gives information on all types of cancer; can refer to appropriate organisations for further help; produces leaflets and educational material including films and video cassettes.

Ulster Cancer Foundation (Cancer Information Service)
40–42 Eglantine Avenue
Belfast
Telephone: 0232 663439

Supports and informs the public and health professionals in all areas of concern related to cancer problems; operated by experienced cancer nurses; literature available.